THE BEST OF BROCHURE DESIGN 10

PERRY CHUA

ROCKPORT PUBLISHERS
BEVERLY MASSACHUSETTS

CONTENTS

First published in the United States of America by
Rockport Publishers, a member of
Quayside Publishing Group
100 Cummings Center
Suite 406-L
Beverly, Massachusetts 01915-6101
Telephone: (978) 282-9590
Fax: (978) 283-2742
www.rockpub.com

Library of Congress Cataloging-in-Publication Data
Chua, Perry.
The best of brochure design 10 / Perry Chua.
p. cm.
ISBN 978-1-59253-446-3
1. Brochures--Design. I. Title. II. Title: Best of brochure design ten.
Z246.5.B76C48 2008
686--dc22
2008023505
CIP

Paperback edition published 2009

ISBN-13: 978-1-59253-628-3
ISBN-10: 1-59253-628-x

10 9 8 7 6 5 4 3 2 1

Design
Perry Chua
perrychua.com

Production
Jason Pavich - Manager
Simon West - Assistant

Photography
Thomas Billingsley
thomasbillingsley.com

Cover Illustration
Adrien Van Viersen

Printed in Singapore

PREFACE

Can you judge a brochure by its cover? Well, yes, you often can.

A brochure is a lot like a person. Each is different; every one has something to say. The brochure cover, for example, has to do a good job of introducing itself, as if to say, "You might want to listen to this and here's why." If the cover can compel the reader to pick it up and open it, a major hurdle has been overcome.

Next comes the chance to communicate. Through pictures and words—and everything in between—the brochure tells its story to the reader compellingly and with relevance. It should hold their interest until they are ready to do, think, or even feel what you want them to.

The selected entries featured here were judged on many different levels, among them effective use of typography, design, and craftsmanship. But, like the hallmarks of any successful brochure, winning entries hold one thing in common: outstanding pick-up appeal. And like a good book, we found them impossible to put down. Each virtually jumped into our hands and drove us to explore page by page, line by line, and image by image. And every one had its own story to tell.

At times, I have feared that the printed brochure would be to the digital age what the horse and cart was to the automobile. But, in reviewing submissions from around the globe, I became convinced of the staying power of good design on paper. Far from a selection of "paper salesmen," what you see in these pages is an integral part of a design system—one that allows the expression of brand vision by eloquently articulating brand character.

To all those who contributed, I offer congratulations and a heartfelt thank you. You made this book possible. With over 1400 entries received from 28 countries, some 200 entries were selected for inclusion. I am truly honored to be a part of this remarkable collection of design excellence. I hope you enjoy the outcome as much as I enjoyed the process.

Perry Chua

★ IN THIS SECTION

DESIGN ARMY

RAMP

DESIGN DEPOT

WECHSLER

CARRÉNOIR ROMA

HANGAR 18 CREATIVE GROUP

PETRICK DESIGN

THE JUPITER DRAWING ROOM

PHILOGRAPHICA, INC.

SALTERBAXTER

ANNUAL REPORTS

★ **DESIGN ARMY** | ART DIRECTOR **PUM LEFEBURE, JAKE LEFEBURE** | DESIGNER **MIKE MALUSO**
CLIENT **BLACK BOOK PUBLISHING** | PAPER/MATERIALS **FINCH FINE**

DESIGN ARMY | ART DIRECTOR **PUM LEFEBURE, JAKE LEFEBURE** | DESIGNER **MIKE MALUSO** ★
CLIENT **BLACK BOOK PUBLISHING** | PAPER/MATERIALS **FINCH FINE**

...ch embraced the life of our late Char...
...owever his materials were scanty, & reg...
...him. of the Mentor of my youth I felt th...
...witnesses to his virtues, and furnished...
...tely he sent me his 1st. vol. and indeed...
...ly written; exhibiting mind, informe...
...o florid perhaps for the sober style of...
however he had a great example in...
also a little too speculative, in which...
...ndulge with the brevity of Tacitus. as it is...
apply to me as to other characters of hi...
...mmunications may be delicate, it...
...know something more of him. what is...
...d political, does he write for money or...
...ation as to these particulars must go...
...ces, and with a view to regulate them...
...r of your information, with an assur...
...used for no other purpose, and th...
...hall be burnt the moment it is [illegible]...
...ks for this kind office accept my [illegible]...

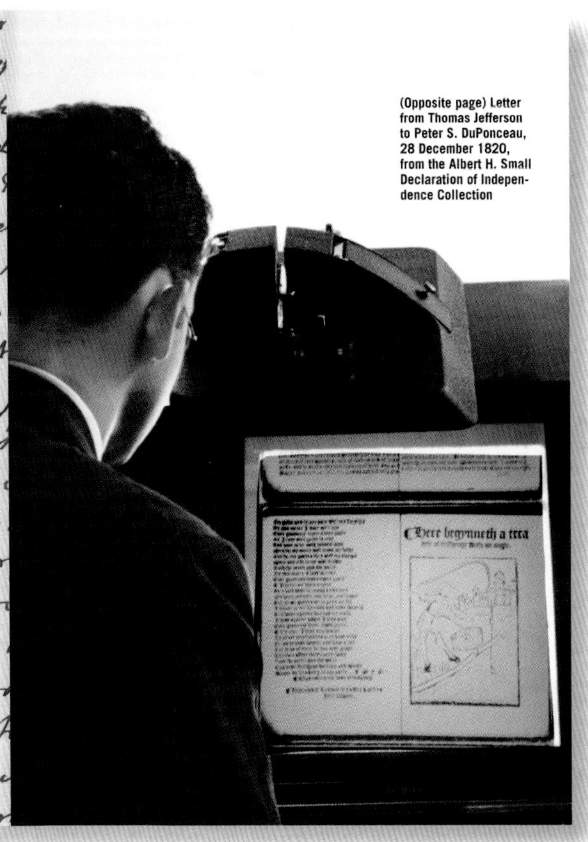

(Opposite page) Letter from Thomas Jefferson to Peter S. DuPonceau, 28 December 1820, from the Albert H. Small Declaration of Independence Collection

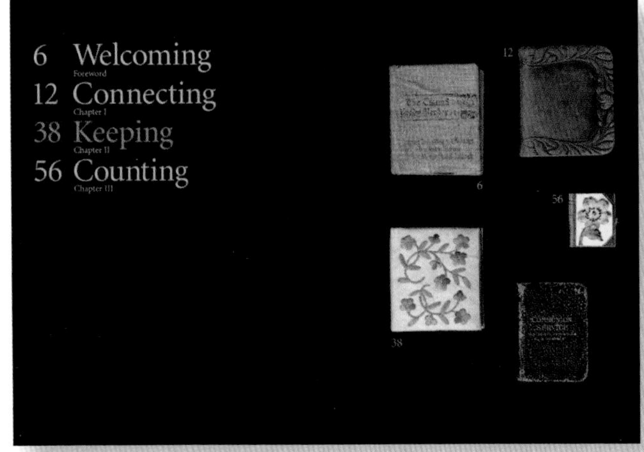

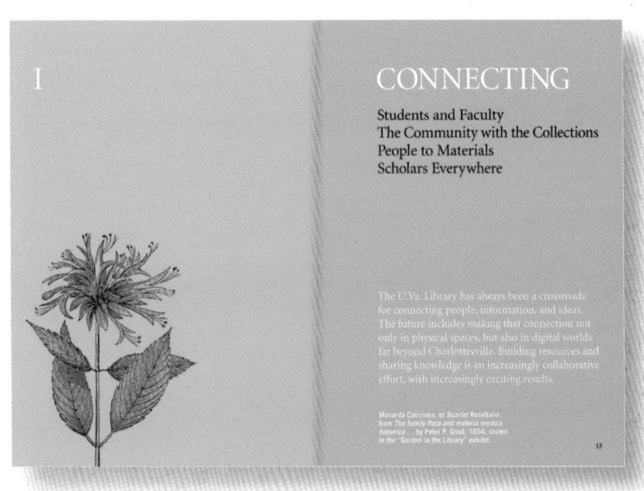

★ **RAMP** | ART DIRECTOR **MICHAEL STINSON** | DESIGNER **CLAIRE DE LÉON, ANGELA KIM**
CLIENT **CWS CAPITAL PARTNERS, LLC** | PAPER/MATERIALS **WEYERHAEUSER COUGAR OPAQUE VELLUM 80 LB. TEXT**

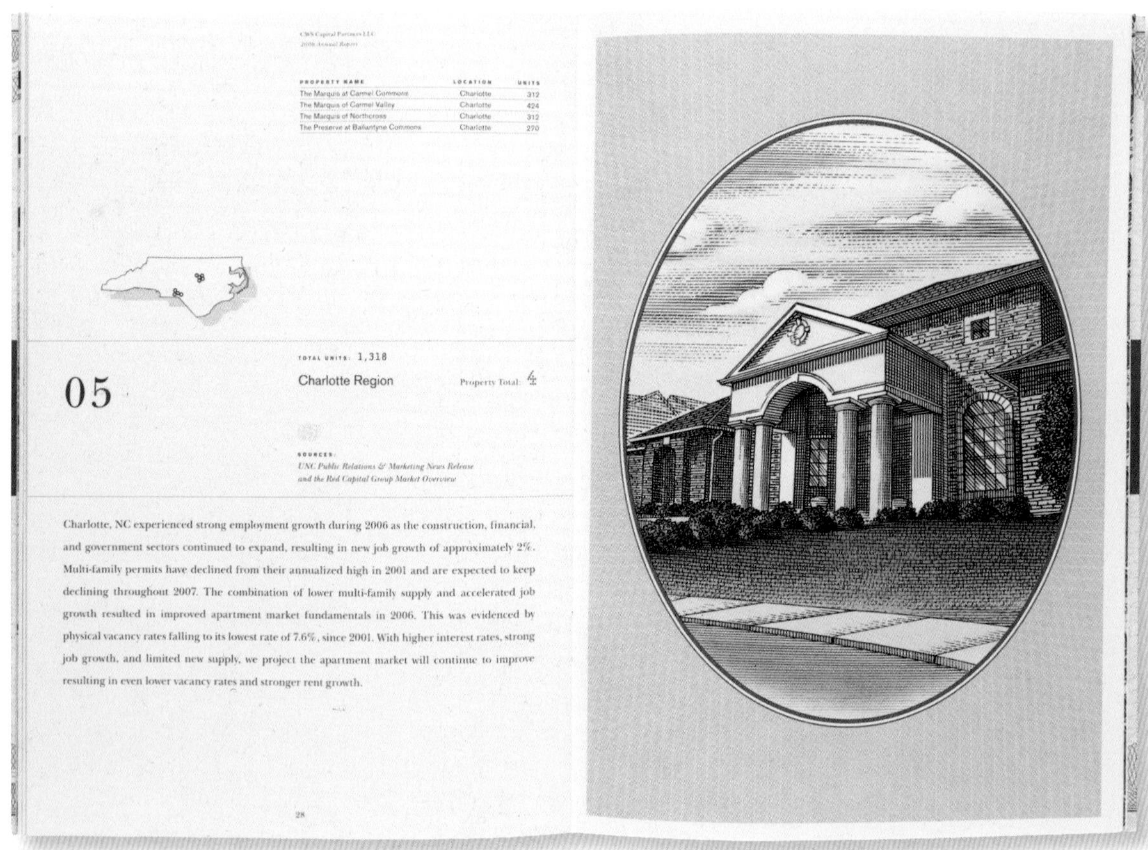

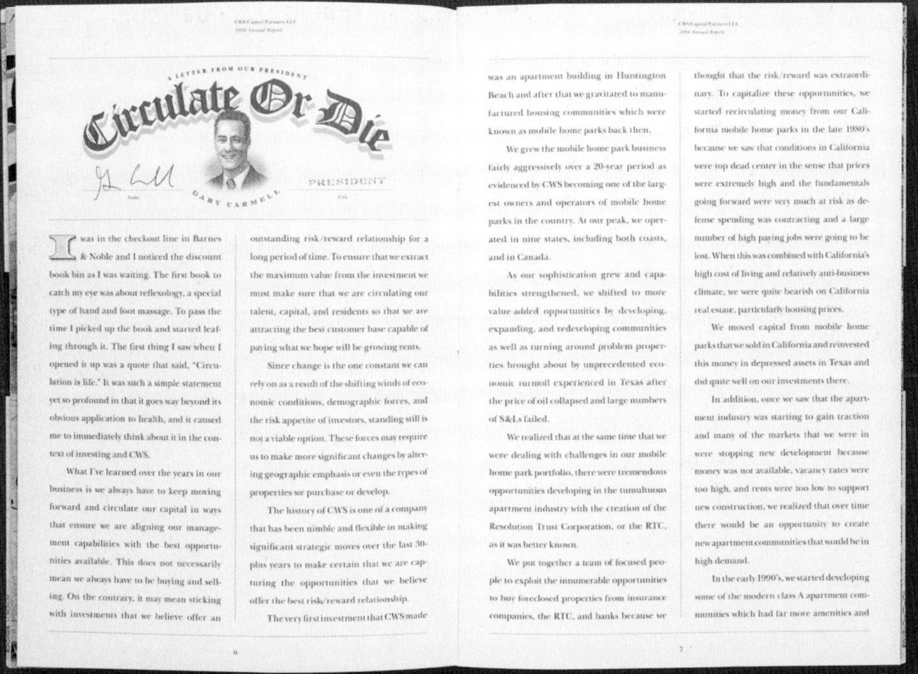

CWS Capital Partners LLC
2006 Annual Report

A LETTER FROM OUR PRESIDENT

Circulate Or Die

Name GARY CARMELL PRESIDENT Title

I was in the checkout line in Barnes & Noble and I noticed the discount book bin as I was waiting. The first book to catch my eye was about reflexology, a special type of hand and foot massage. To pass the time I picked up the book and started leafing through it. The first thing I saw when I opened it up was a quote that said, "Circulation is life." It was such a simple statement yet so profound in that it goes way beyond its obvious application to health, and it caused me to immediately think about it in the context of investing and CWS.

What I've learned over the years in our business is we always have to keep moving forward and circulate our capital in ways that ensure we are aligning our management capabilities with the best opportunities available. This does not necessarily mean we always have to be buying and selling. On the contrary, it may mean sticking with investments that we believe offer an outstanding risk/reward relationship for a long period of time. To ensure that we extract the maximum value from the investment we must make sure that we are circulating our talent, capital, and residents so that we are attracting the best customer base capable of paying what we hope will be growing rents.

Since change is the one constant we can rely on as a result of the shifting winds of economic conditions, demographic forces, and the risk appetite of investors, standing still is not a viable option. These forces may require us to make more significant changes by altering geographic emphasis or even the types of properties we purchase or develop.

The history of CWS is one of a company that has been nimble and flexible in making significant strategic moves over the last 30-plus years to make certain that we are capturing the opportunities that we believe offer the best risk/reward relationship.

The very first investment that CWS made

6

CWS Capital Partners LLC
2006 Annual Report

was an apartment building in Huntington Beach and after that we gravitated to manufactured housing communities which were known as mobile home parks back then.

We grew the mobile home park business fairly aggressively over a 20-year period as evidenced by CWS becoming one of the largest owners and operators of mobile home parks in the country. At our peak, we operated in nine states, including both coasts, and in Canada.

As our sophistication grew and capabilities strengthened, we shifted to more value added opportunities by developing, expanding, and redeveloping communities as well as turning around problem properties brought about by unprecedented economic turmoil experienced in Texas after the price of oil collapsed and large numbers of S&Ls failed.

We realized that at the same time that we were dealing with challenges in our mobile home park portfolio, there were tremendous opportunities developing in the tumultuous apartment industry with the creation of the Resolution Trust Corporation, or the RTC, as it was better known.

We put together a team of focused people to exploit the innumerable opportunities to buy foreclosed properties from insurance companies, the RTC, and banks because we thought that the risk/reward was extraordinary. To capitalize these opportunities, we started recirculating money from our California mobile home parks in the late 1980's because we saw that conditions in California were top dead center in the sense that prices were extremely high and the fundamentals going forward were very much at risk as defense spending was contracting and a large number of high paying jobs were going to be lost. When this was combined with California's high cost of living and relatively anti-business climate, we were quite bearish on California real estate, particularly housing prices.

We moved capital from mobile home parks that we sold in California and reinvested this money in depressed assets in Texas and did quite well on our investments there.

In addition, once we saw that the apartment industry was starting to gain traction and many of the markets that we were in were stopping new development because money was not available, vacancy rates were too high, and rents were too low to support new construction, we realized that over time there would be an opportunity to create new apartment communities that would be in high demand.

In the early 1990's, we started developing some of the modern class A apartment communities which had far more amenities and

7

LETTER TO THE Investors WRITTEN BY THE FIVE PARTNERS

No 2006

CWS

STEVEN J. SH

0414197605

Annual Report

Real Estate Investment Specialists

(Newport Beach)

CREATED CIRCA 1969

CWS CAPITAL PARTNERS CIRCULATING VALUE EST. 1969

MMVI

President

Chief Executive Officer

2006 2006 2006 2006 2006 2006 2006 2006 2006 2006 2006 2006

★ **DESIGN DEPOT** | ART DIRECTOR **BANKOV PITER** | DESIGNER **EUGENY MALYSHEV** | CLIENT **SOGAZ**

RUSSIA

WECHSLER | ART DIRECTOR **MIKE HALL** | DESIGNER **MIKE HALL, SUE ROBERTSON** | CLIENT **ARCAPITA** ★
PAPER/MATERIALS **IKONO SILK**

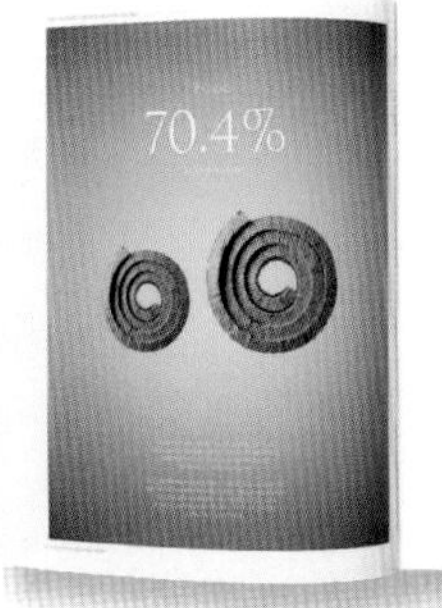

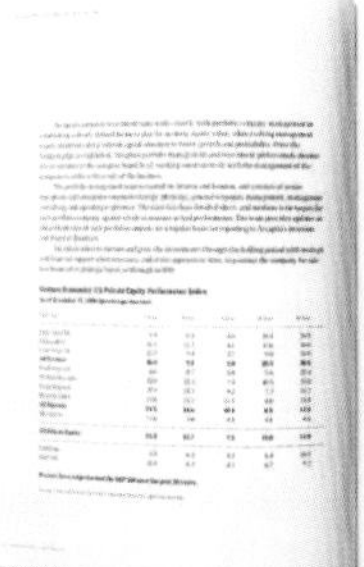

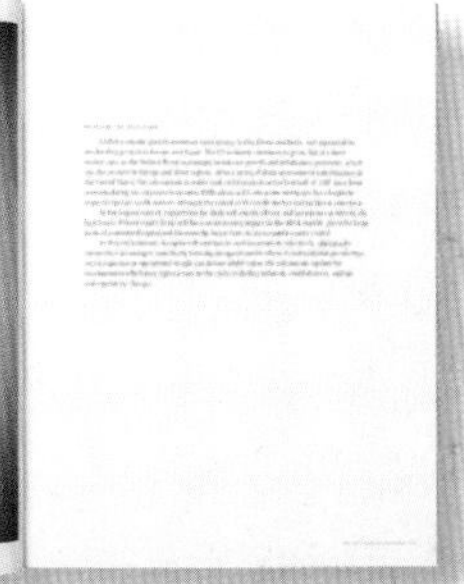
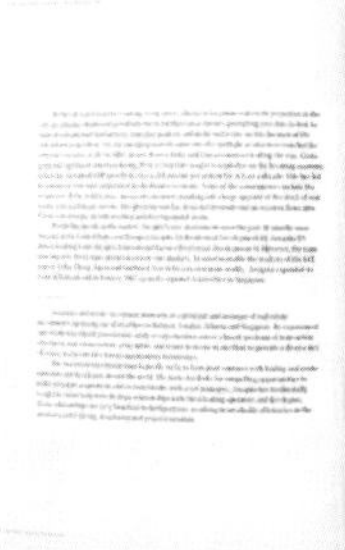

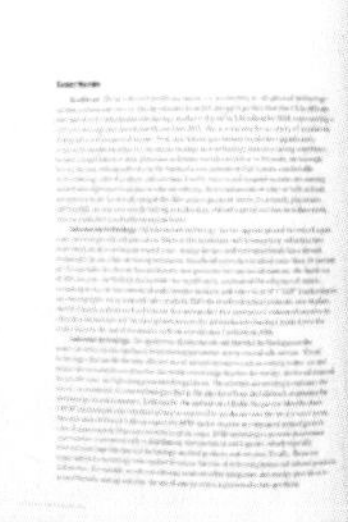
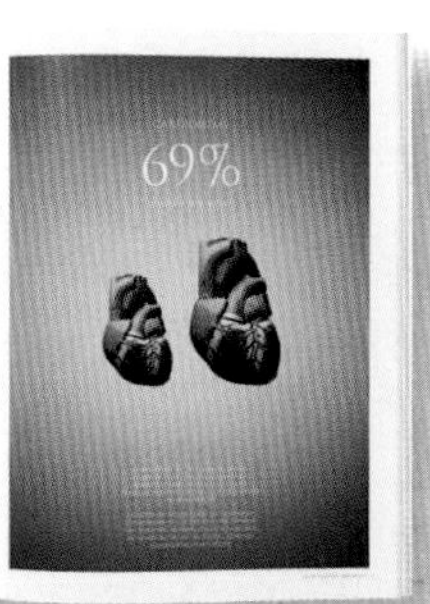

★ **CARRÉNOIR ROMA** | ART DIRECTOR **MASSIMILIANO SAGRATI** | DESIGNER **ALFREDO LANEVE**
CLIENT **FINMECCANICA**

69

4. Andamento della gestione nei settori di attività

Principali dati

Energia

ELICOTTERI | AERONAUTICA | SPAZIO | ELETTRONICA PER LA DIFESA E SICUREZZA | SISTEMI DI DIFESA | ENERGIA E TRASPORTI

22% 15% 6% 29% 9% 19%

IL GRUPPO

★ **HANGAR 18 CREATIVE GROUP** | ART DIRECTOR **KIM WOLF** | DESIGNER **KIM WOLF**
CLIENT **VANCOUVER INTERNATIONAL AIRPORT**

PETRICK DESIGN | ART DIRECTOR **ROBERT PETRICK** | DESIGNER **JEF ANDERSON** | CLIENT **COVANTA HOLDING CORP.** ★
PAPER/MATERIALS **NEENAH ENVIRONMENT PC100–WHITE, SMOOTH 80 LB. COVER AND 100 LB. TEXT, WRAP: CT1, GLAMA NATURAL RECYCLED, 36 LB.**

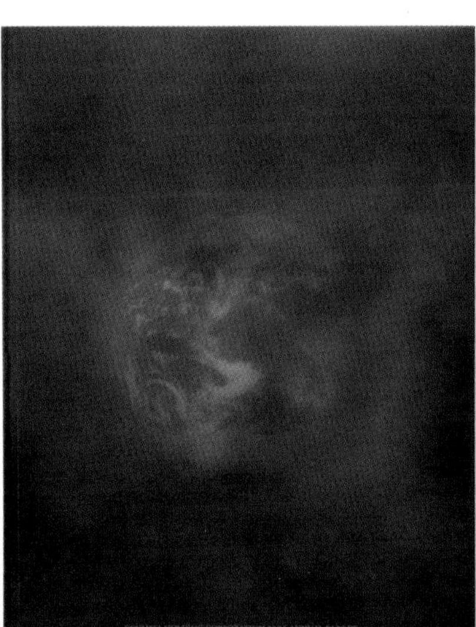

USA

★ **THE JUPITER DRAWING ROOM** | DESIGNER **ASHRAF MAJIE, WASEEMA SURHADIA** | CLIENT **SANLAM**
PAPER/MATERIALS **AVALON MATTE**

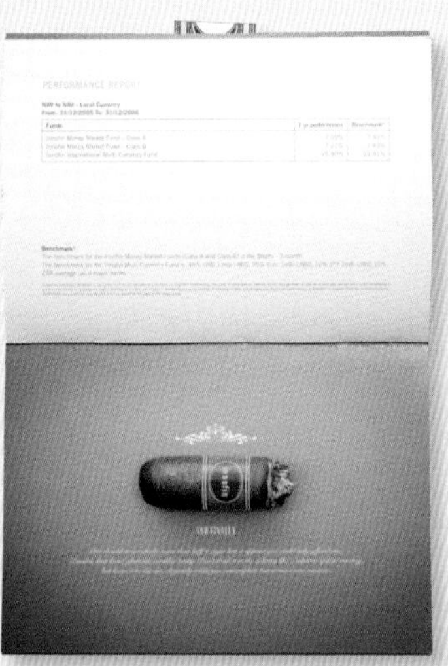

PHILOGRAPHICA, INC. | ART DIRECTOR **DAVID HORTON** | DESIGNER **AMY LEBOW** | CLIENT **AQUENT** | PAPER/MATERIALS **MOHAWK OPTIONS VELLUM**

★

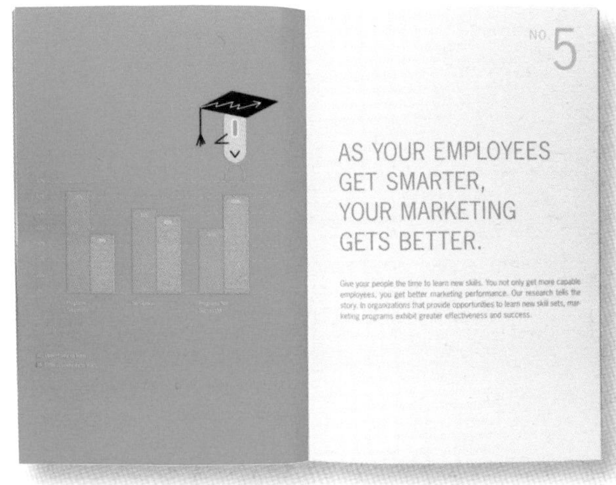

★ **RAMP** | ART DIRECTOR **RACHEL ELNAR, MICHAEL STINSON** | DESIGNER **CLAIRE DE LÉON**
CLIENT **EDWARDS LIFESCIENCES** | PAPER/MATERIALS **WEYERHAEUSER COUGAR OPAQUE**

USA

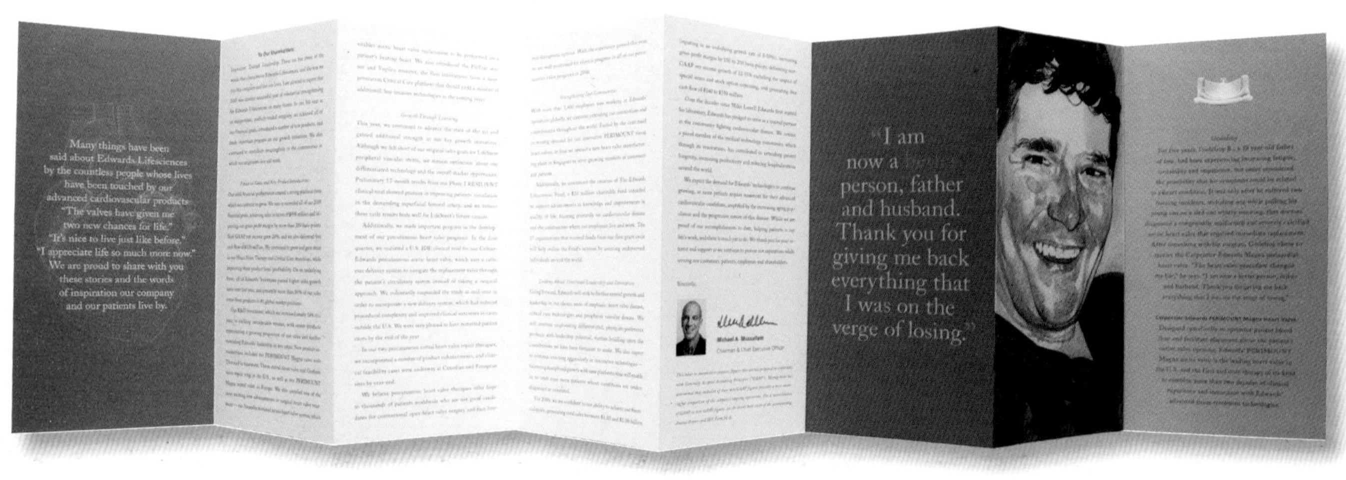

SALTERBAXTER | ART DIRECTOR **JAMES WILSON** | DESIGNER **ALAN DELGADO** ★
CLIENT **ERNST & YOUNG** | PAPER/MATERIALS **REVIVE**

01

Our profession continues to change, but today we have a clear picture of where it is going and how we must adapt – and our achievements this year demonstrate this. The business world as a whole has adjusted well to the increased economic and political uncertainties of the past several years and demand for the quality services that we provide has been high.

In the UK, during our 2004-2005 financial year, each of our service lines grew and we increased our overall gross fee income by 15%, to £945m, with an average profit per partner of £561k.

On the following two pages I answer some of the most important questions Ernst & Young faces.

★ **SALTERBAXTER** | ART DIRECTOR **JAMES WILSON** | DESIGNER **ROSE TOMLINSON** | CLIENT **LAND SECURITIES**
PAPER/MATERIALS **CHALLENGER OFFSET**

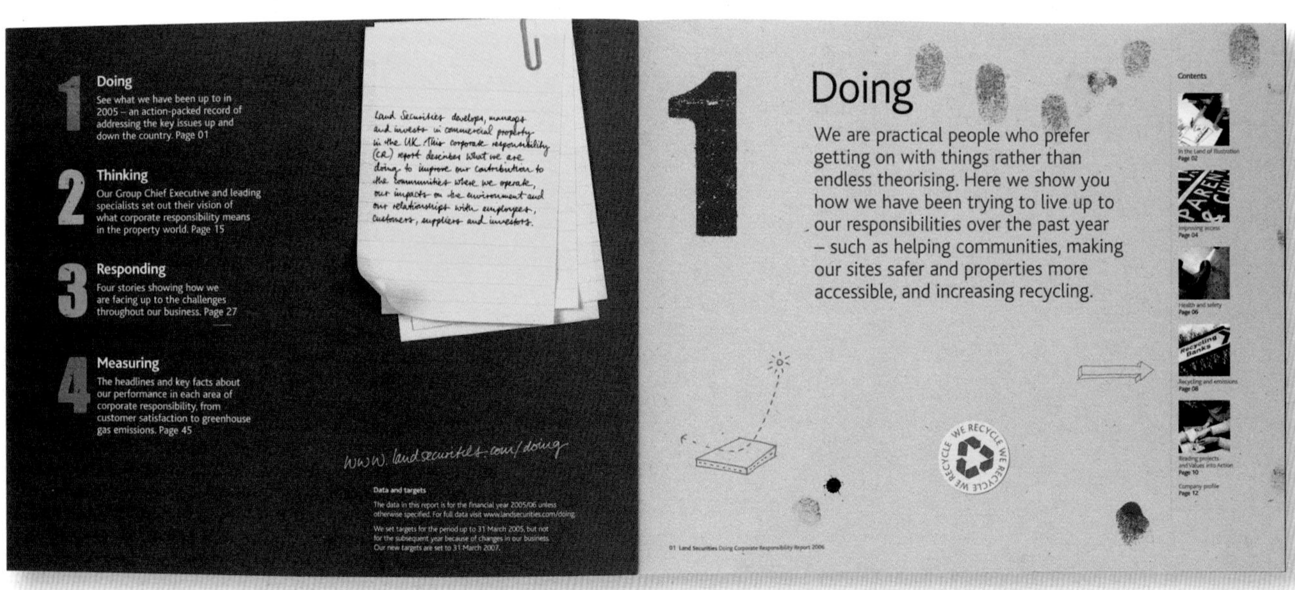

SALTERBAXTER | ART DIRECTOR **JAMES WILSON** | DESIGNER **NINA PICKUP** | CLIENT **ALLEN & OVERY** ★
PAPER/MATERIALS **NEPTUNE UNIQUE**

★ IN THIS SECTION

CORPORATE

★ **DESIGN DEPOT** | ART DIRECTOR **BANKOV PITER** | DESIGNER **EUGENY MALYSHEV** | CLIENT **OSTAFYEVO**

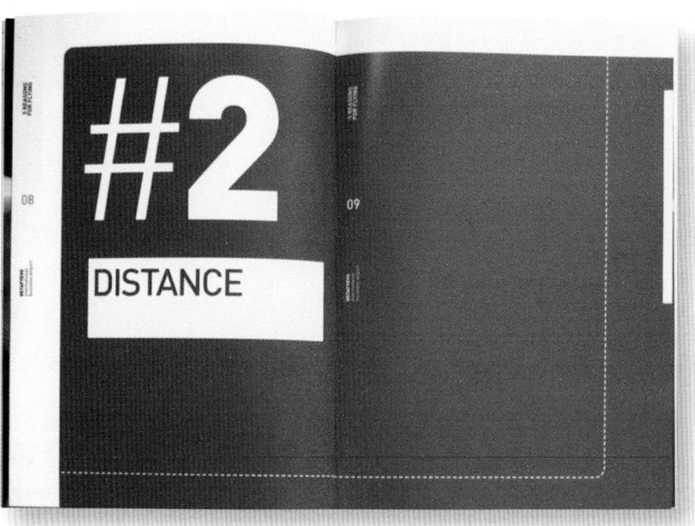

ALWAYS A CLEAR SKY

We wish you a nice flight and anticipate to see you in Ostafyevo

THIS IS WHO WE ARE. OUR GREATEST CAPITAL IS INTELLECTUAL: US. OUR MINDS AND HOW WE APPLY THEM. TOGETHER, EACH DAY, TO MAKE OUR CUSTOMERS' NETWORKS OPERATE AT REDUCED RISKS AND INCREASED OPERATING RATIOS.

MASTERMINDING RAIL TRANSPORTATION.

ANSALDO STS REPRESENTS OUR INTEGRATION WORLDWIDE.

OUR SIGNALLING AND TRANSPORT SYSTEMS ACTIVITIES MERGED TO HELP US WIN MORE CONTRACTS IN A GLOBAL MARKET THAT DEMANDS A MORE COMPLETE, INTEGRATED, YET LOCAL APPROACH.

CARRÉNOIR ROMA | ART DIRECTOR **MASSIMILIANO SAGRATI** | DESIGNER **EMANUELA CAPPELLI** ★
CLIENT **ANSALDO STS** | PAPER/MATERIALS **ANTALIS EDITME SOFT WHITE**

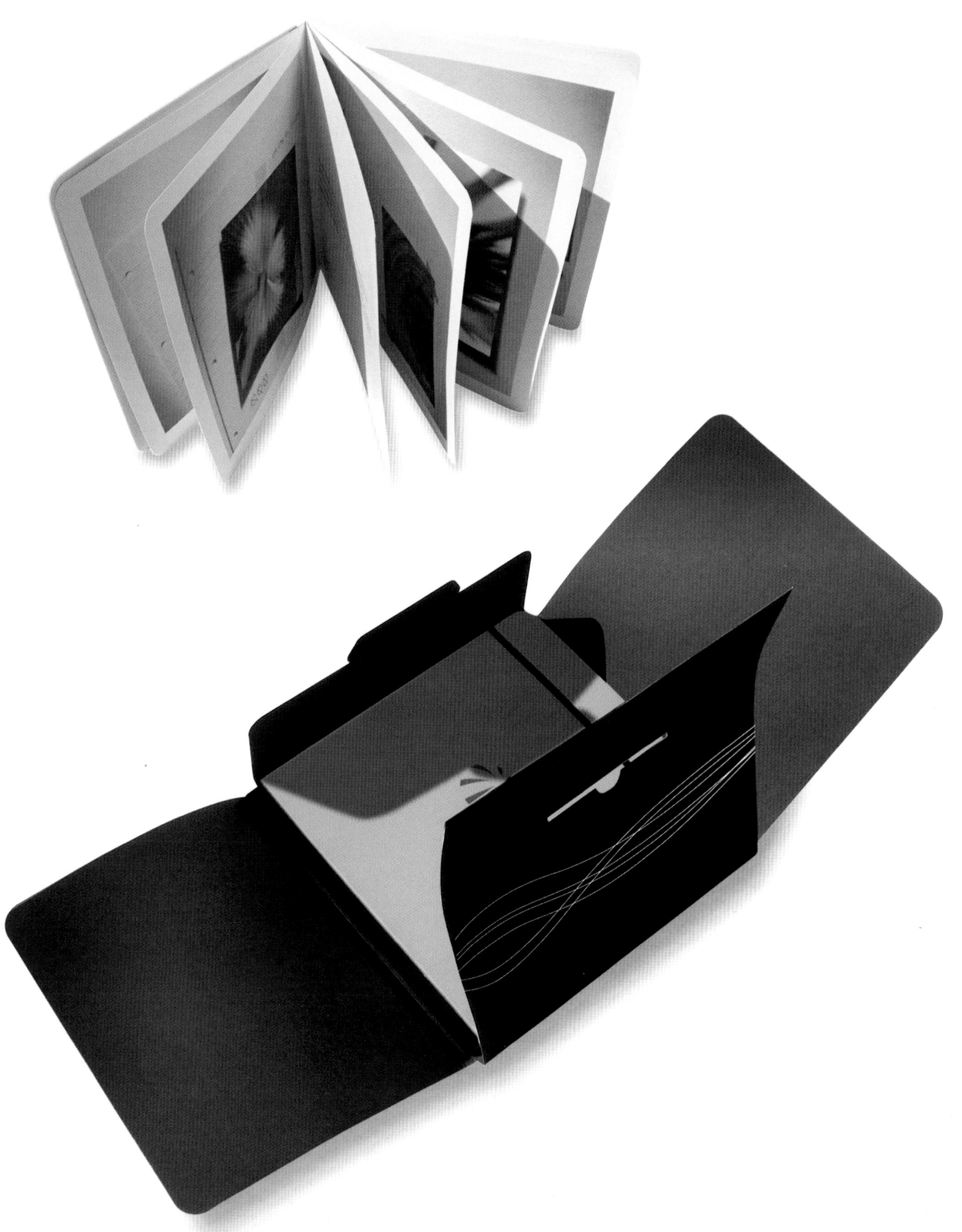

★ **DESIGN ARMY** | ART DIRECTOR **PUM LEFEBURE, JAKE LEFEBURE** | DESIGNER **DAN ADLER** | CLIENT **AMERICAN INSTITUTE OF GRAPHIC ARTS, WASHINGTON DC CHAPTER** | PAPER/MATERIALS **MOHAWK SUPERFINE, FOIL STAMPING**

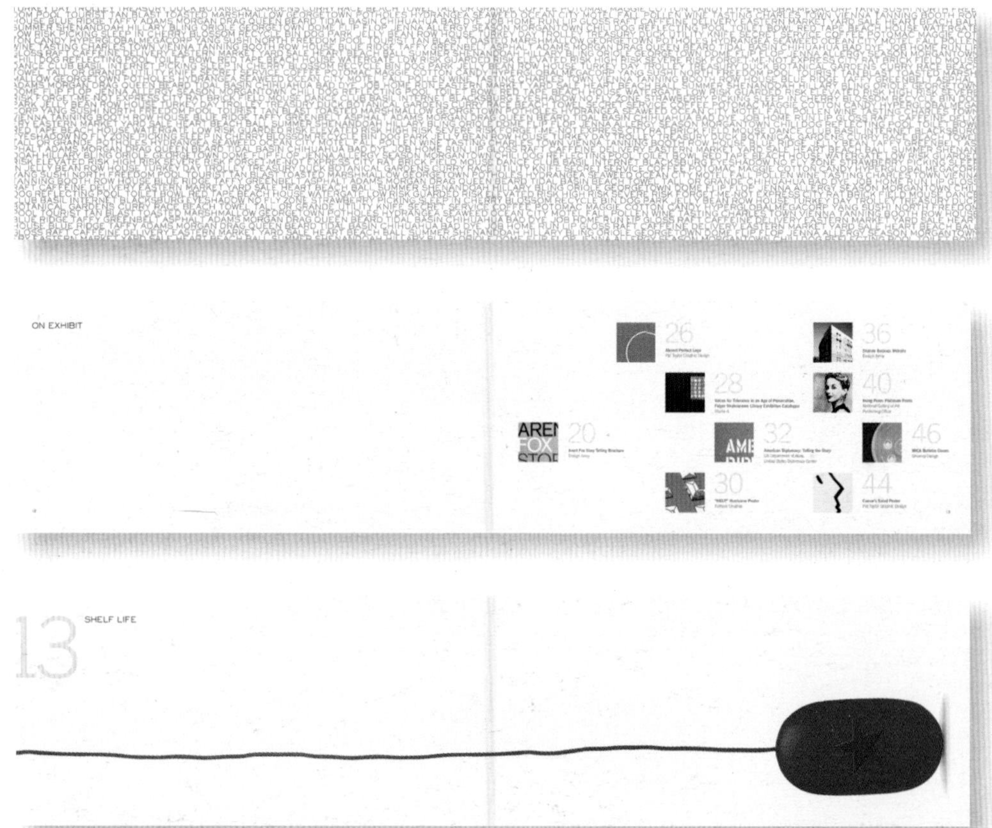

PAPA INC. | ART DIRECTOR **DUBRAVKO PAPA** | DESIGNER **DUBRAVKO PAPA** | CLIENT **GEOFOTO D.O.O.** ★
PAPER/MATERIALS **MUNKEN POLAR, ANTISTATIC BAG**

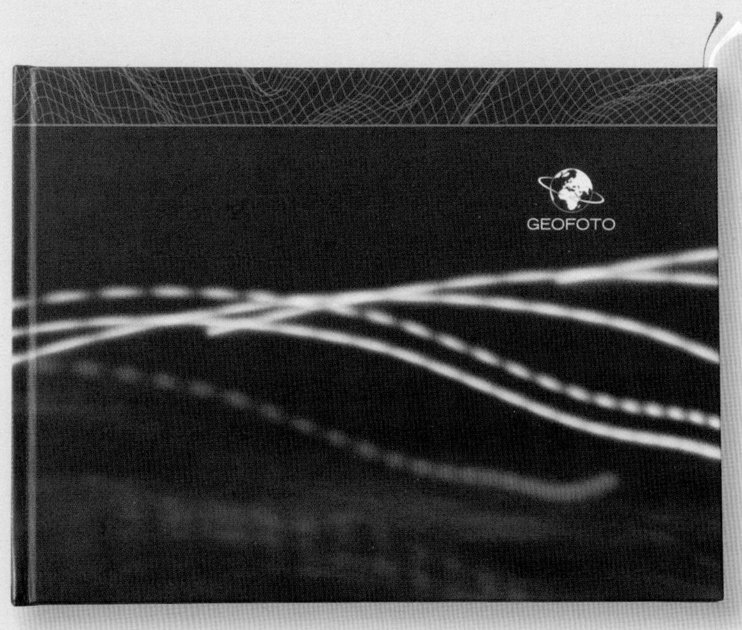

★ **WECHSLER** | ART DIRECTOR **MIKE HALL** | DESIGNER **SUE ROBERTSON, AARON SHAW** | CLIENT **TDR CAPITAL**
PAPER/MATERIALS **NATURALIS AND CURIOUS TRANSLUCENT CLEAR**

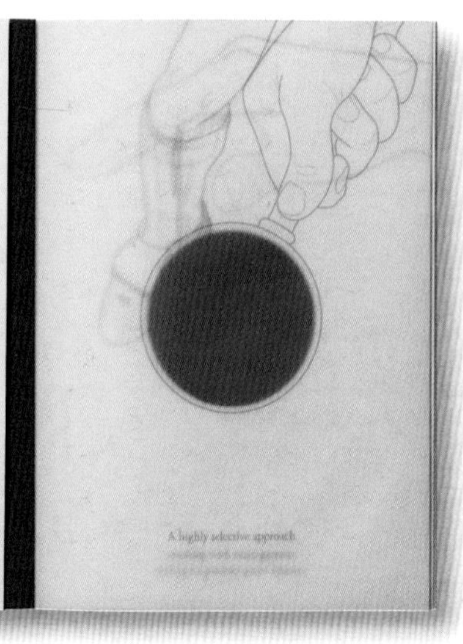

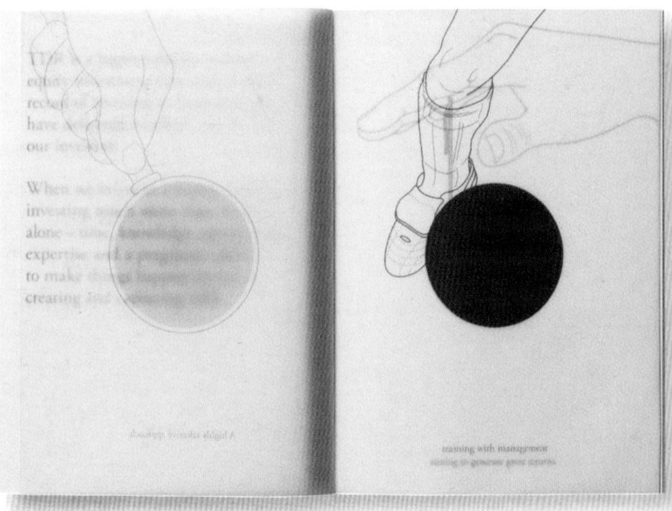

THE JUPITER DRAWING ROOM | DESIGNER **BRANDT BOTES** | CLIENT **SANLAM** ★
PAPER/MATERIALS **MAGNO MATTE AND CROMATICA**

★ **THE JUPITER DRAWING ROOM** | DESIGNER **BRANDT BOTES** | CLIENT **SANLAM**
PAPER/MATERIALS **200 GSM EURO MATTE ART**

RYSZARD BIENERT | ART DIRECTOR **RYSZARD BIENERT** | DESIGNER **RYSZARD BIENERT** | CLIENT **GALERIA PIEKARY 5** ★
PAPER/MATERIALS **COVER: 2 MM CARDBOARD, UV SPOT VARNISH, TEXT: UNCOATED OFFSET PAPER**

★ **BLIK** | ART DIRECTOR **TYLER BLIK** | DESIGNER **KAY TODA** | CLIENT **SGPA ARCHITECTURE + PLANNING**

S DESIGN INC. | ART DIRECTOR **SARAH SEARS** | DESIGNER **MARK BOSTIAN** | CLIENT **INTERSTATE OIL AND GAS COMPACT COMMISSION** | PAPER/MATERIALS **FRENCH DUROTONE** ★

THIS IS OUR CHANCE

Introduction

Before addressing the issue of how to assure the future supply of petroleum professions, it is important to put the dilemma into context.

The oil shocks of the 1970s and 1980s and the subsequent collapse in world energy prices from 1984 to 1986 resulted in a major retrenchment of the energy industry. The domestic industry alone lost more than a half million jobs in the mid-1980s. Subsequent to the price collapse that culminated in 1986, the industry has experienced substantial volatility in energy prices that has posed special challenges to maintaining a stable workforce. The price volatility continues today.

Investment in new infrastructure, refineries and other critical facilities for delivery of energy to the global economy has dropped significantly since the 1980s. This dramatic slowdown in investment has caused a large reduction in the excess delivery capacity that the industry traditionally had maintained. This loss of excess capacity is to blame, in part, for the recent spikes in prices that have occurred as the industry struggles to meet market demand in the growing global economy.

In addition, proprietary research and development (R&D) by the major operating companies were reduced dramatically as part of the austerity mindset that major operators were forced to adopt. Operators shifted from programs of highly competitive, proprietary R&D to a reliance on outside technology developed by service companies and universities. However, the funding cuts imposed by the industry during this period also affected the programs at universities and service companies and caused many of these programs to fall into ill health as well. In the same period, government-funded energy R&D also came under pressure, and dramatic reductions in federal spending made an already serious problem even worse. Federal spending continues to decline from a low level to ever lower levels. Dramatic changes in employment demographics of the energy industry then emerged. The industry hired aggressively from 1974 to 1983, and built up large staffs. Many of these people lost their jobs in the mid-1980s. In following years, those who stayed in the industry have witnessed a seemingly unending process of layoffs, reorganizations, mergers and consolidation. The "survivors," who are a large part of the current employment base of the industry, are now

★ **HELENA SEO DESIGN** | ART DIRECTOR **HELENA SEO** | DESIGNER **HELENA SEO** | CLIENT **VIVENDI DEVELOPMENT**
PAPER/MATERIALS **STARWHITE SIRIUS SMOOTH, 130 LB. DTC, CENTURA MATTE TEXT, 100 LB.**

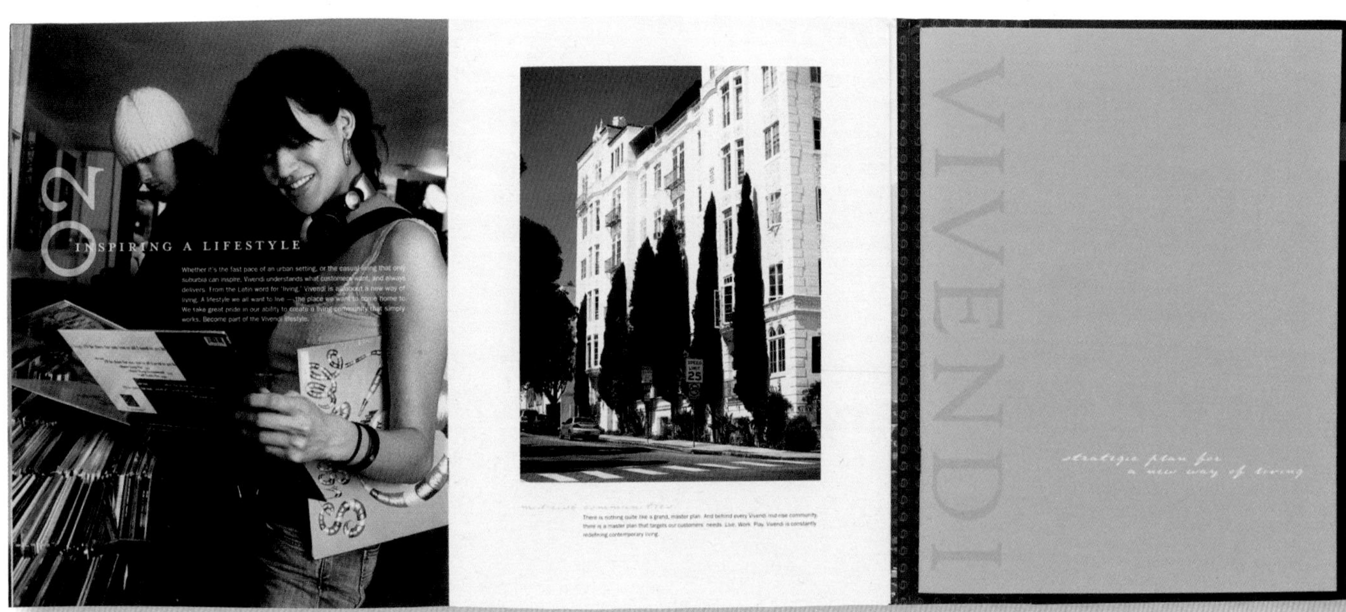

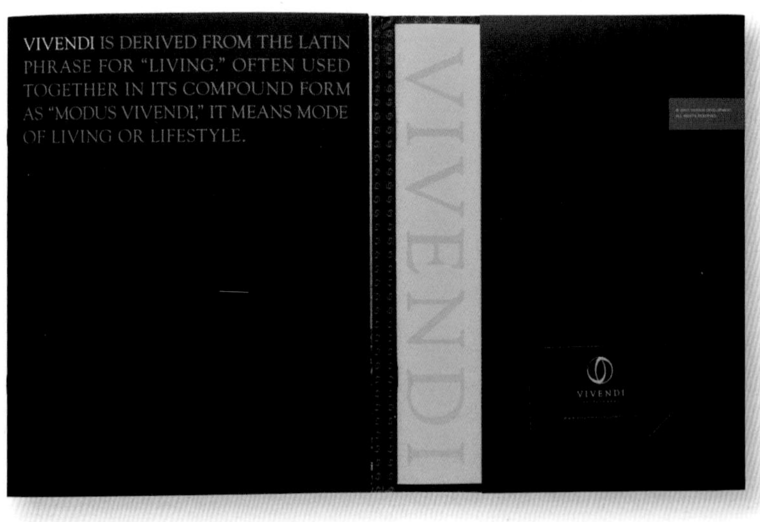

RENEE RECH DESIGN | ART DIRECTOR **RENEE RECH** | DESIGNER **RENEE RECH** | CLIENT **BANANA REPUBLIC** ★
PAPER/MATERIALS **SMART PAPER: CARNIVAL COVER (COCO & SKY), NEENAH ENVIRONMENT TEXT, VELLUM-REICH PAPER, RIVETS, FOIL STAMPING, LEATHER CORD**

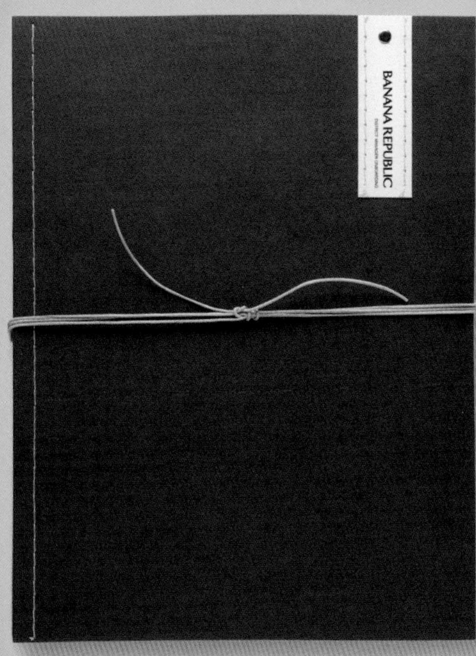

★ **SIMON & GOETZ DESIGN** | ART DIRECTOR **BERND VOLLMÖLLER** | DESIGNER **BERND VOLLMÖLLER**
CLIENT **SAL. OPPENHEIM JR. & CIE. KGAA** | PAPER/MATERIALS **GALAXI SUPERMAT, GALAXI KERAMIK**

Leben ohne Grenzen

WIEDER UND WIEDER SUCHEN SIE DAS ABENTEUER – DIE GROSSEN ENTDECKER UND EROBERER UNSERES PLANETEN. WAS TREIBT DIESE MENSCHEN AN?

Freiheit

Im Kern ist Freiheit die Abwesenheit von Zwang bei der Wahl von Handlungsalternativen. Heute wird grundsätzlich zwischen „negativer Freiheit" – bezogen auf die Pressefreiheit ist darunter beispielsweise die Möglichkeit der freien Meinungsäußerung zu verstehen – und „positiver Freiheit" unterschieden. In letzterem Fall bedeutet dies die Bereitstellung von Kommunikationsmitteln.

Wider die Zwänge

DIE IDEE DER FREIHEIT GERÄT INTELLEKTUELL IMMER MEHR IN DIE DEFENSIVE. EIN GESPRÄCH MIT LORD RALF DAHRENDORF ZUR AKTUELLEN DEBATTE UM EINEN PHILOSOPHISCHEN BEGRIFF.

DIE PHILOSOPHIE DER FREIHEIT BEGANN EINST IN DEM *Bestreben, Sklaverei und Leibeigenschaft abzuschaffen. In der Phase der Aufklärung meinte Freiheit den Ausbruch aus überkommenem Denken und die politische Überwindung vormoderner Strukturen. Ziele waren sowohl die Trennung von Staat und Kirche als auch die Einführung der Gewaltenteilung als Grundlage für Rechtsstaatlichkeit und Demokratie. Gleichzeitig wurde von nun an auch darüber gestritten, wie weit Freiheit gehen dürfe. Mit Begriffen wie Pflicht und Verantwortung wurde die Freiheitsidee ethisch eingegrenzt. Heute wird grundsätzlich zwischen negativer und positiver Freiheit unterschieden. Während unter negativer Freiheit (oder „Freiheit von") zum Beispiel eine zensurfreie Meinungsäußerung verstanden wird, bezieht sich die positive Freiheit (oder „Freiheit zu") auf die Bereitstellung von Kommunikationsmitteln, damit die Meinungsäußerung auch realisiert werden kann.*

Nach der kristallklaren Definition des liberalen Soziologen Lord Ralf Dahrendorf bedeutet Freiheit im Kern die Abwesenheit von Zwang, das heißt die Fähigkeit und den Willen, zu tun und zu lassen, was man möchte. Ein Grundsatz der Freiheit lautet: Je größer die Nichteinmischung, desto größer die persönliche Freiheit. In der praktischen Umsetzung bedarf es jedoch einer Verfassung der Freiheit in Gestalt einer liberalen Ordnung, die strenggenommen eine Limitierung der reinen Freiheit darstellt. Dieser Freiheitsbegriff scheint heute durch Gerechtigkeitspostulate, ökonomische Verkürzungen und Sicherheitsdogmen in die intellektuelle Defensive geraten zu sein. Die aktuellen Bedrohungen der Freiheit haben zugenommen. Wieviel Mut zur Verteidigung ist sie uns noch wert? Darüber unterhielt sich der Publizist Norbert Seitz mit Lord Ralf Dahrendorf.

Ausgehend von der Unterscheidung des britischen Philosophen Isaiah Berlin zwischen „positiver" und „negativer" Freiheit, wäre zu fragen, warum es aus Ihrer Sicht eine „positive" oder „soziale Freiheit" als eine Erweiterung des individuellen Handlungsspielraums durch den Staat nicht geben kann?

LORD DAHRENDORF: Das ist ein Mißbrauch. Wir sollten Dinge nicht beim falschen Namen nennen, und Freiheit ist eines und Gerechtigkeit ist ein anderes. Es gibt sehr wohl soziale Voraussetzungen einer für alle zugänglichen Freiheit. Aber man sollte es nicht Freiheit nennen. Und schon gar nicht sollte man es aufwiegen gegen andere Grundfreiheiten. Anders gesprochen: Freiheit ist Freiheit ist Freiheit, Gerechtigkeit ist Gerechtigkeit ist Gerechtigkeit.

GLOBALISIERUNG

Wie hat sich die Balance zwischen Freiheit und Gerechtigkeit durch die grenzensprengende Globalisierung verschoben?

LORD DAHRENDORF: Die neuen Entwicklungen haben natürlich enorme Freiheitsmöglichkeiten gebracht. Gleichzeitig sind neue Ungleichheiten in einem bislang nicht bekannten Ausmaß entstanden. Die unteren zehn Prozent in den USA haben beispielsweise in ›

CECIL TAYLOR

FREE JAZZ

Vom Traumdrama zum Seifenkitsch

Einschalten und Wohlfühlen

★ **NASSAR DESIGN** | ART DIRECTOR **NELIDA NASSAR** | DESIGNER **NELIDA NASSAR** | CLIENT **HARVARD DESIGN SCHOOL**
PAPER/MATERIALS **TEXT: COUGAR SMOOTH, 80 LB., COVER: COUGAR SMOOTH, 100 LB.**

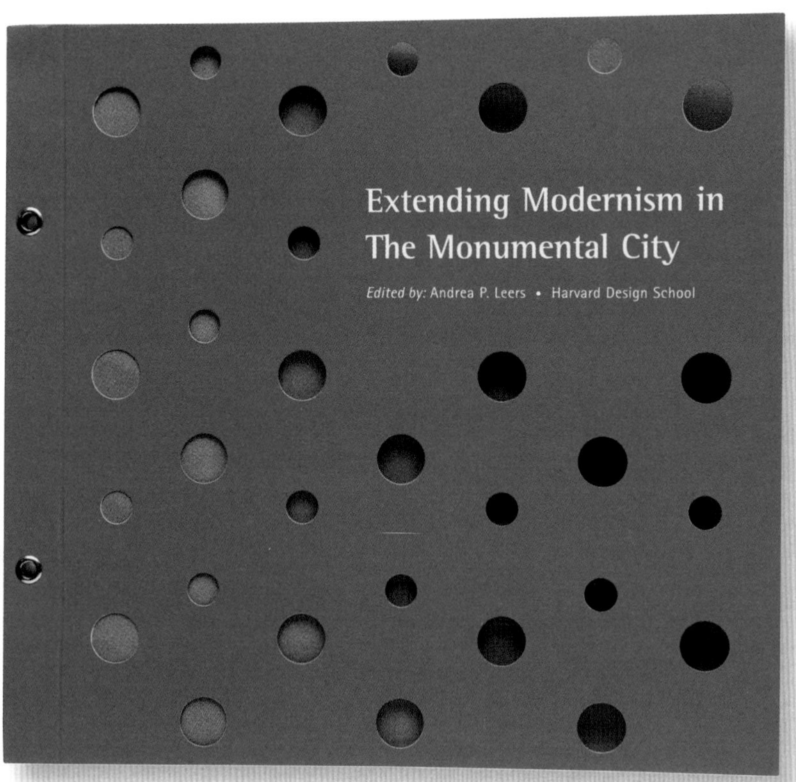

USA

DIE TRANSFORMER | ART DIRECTOR/DESIGNER **MARTIN SCHONHOFF, MICHAEL THEILE** ★

CLIENT **BUNDESVERBAND DRUCK & MEDIEN E.V.** | PAPER/MATERIALS **FLUORESCENT COLOR, DIE CUT, HOT FOIL STAMPING**

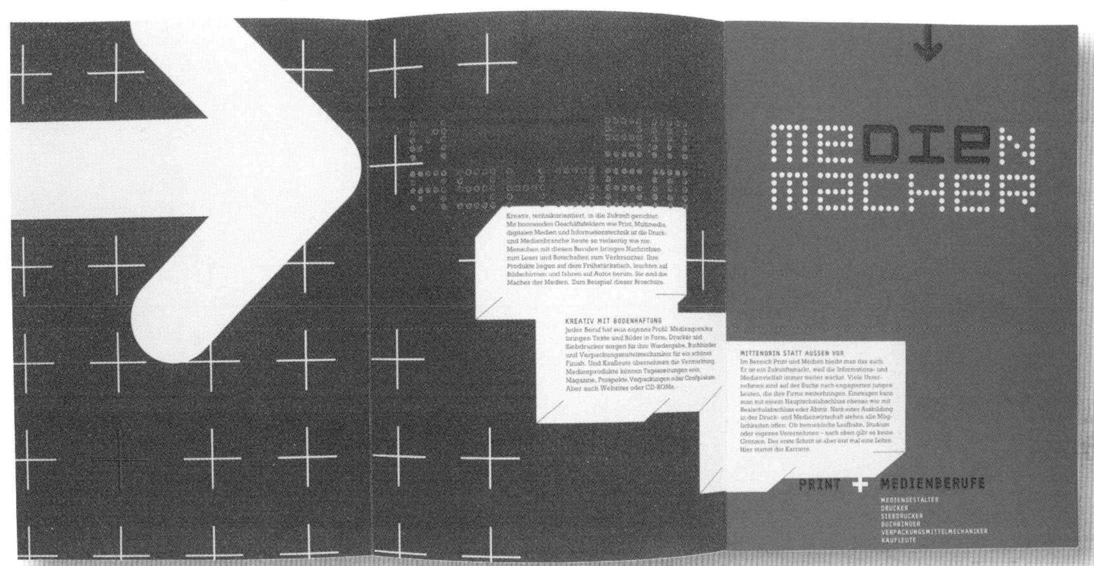

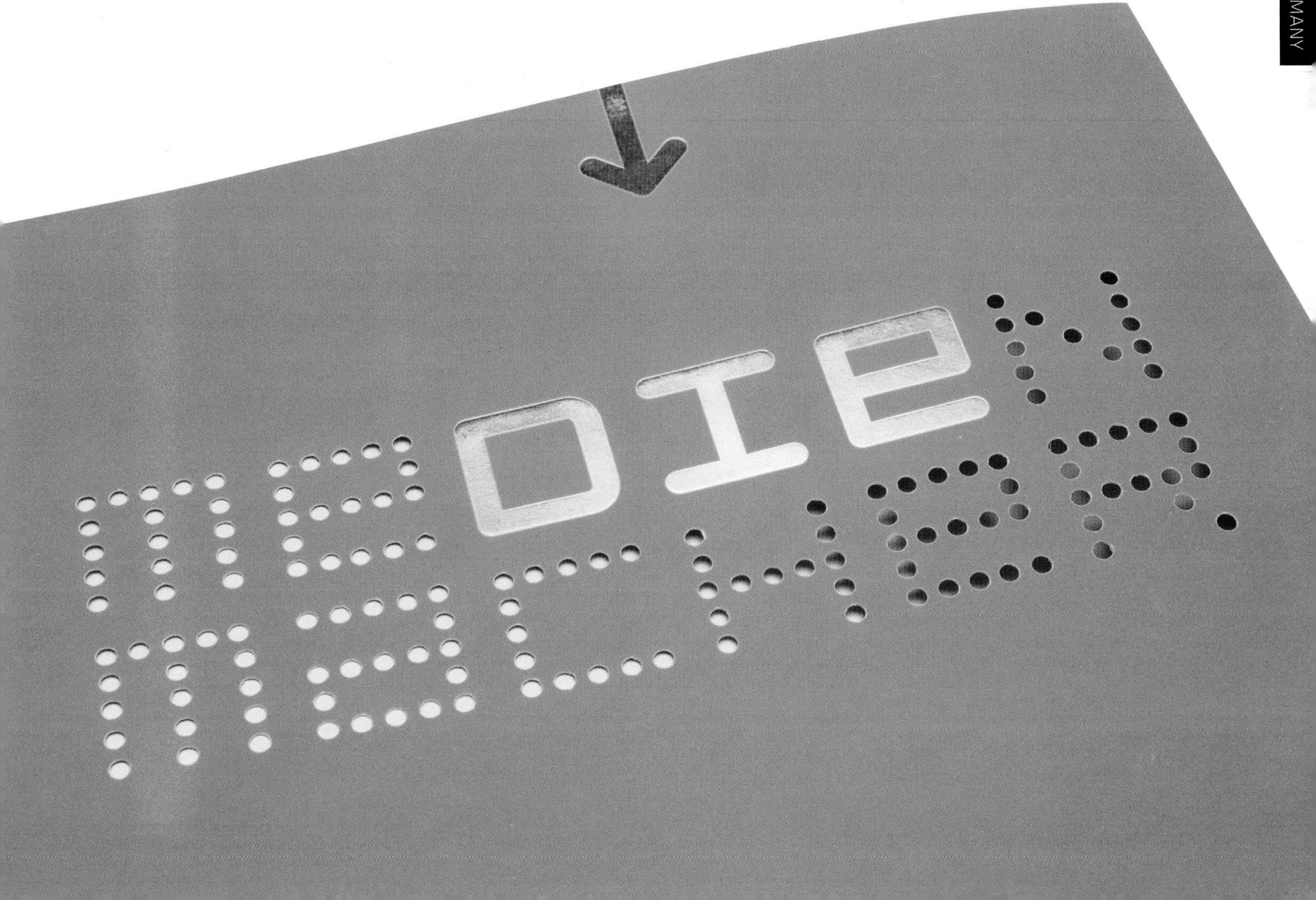

★ **BOCCALATTE** | ART DIRECTOR **SUZANNE BOCCALATTE** | DESIGNER **SUZANNE BOCCALATTE**
CLIENT **CAMPBELLTOWN ART CENTRE** | PAPER/MATERIALS **MEGA GLOSS, OPTICS YELLOW**

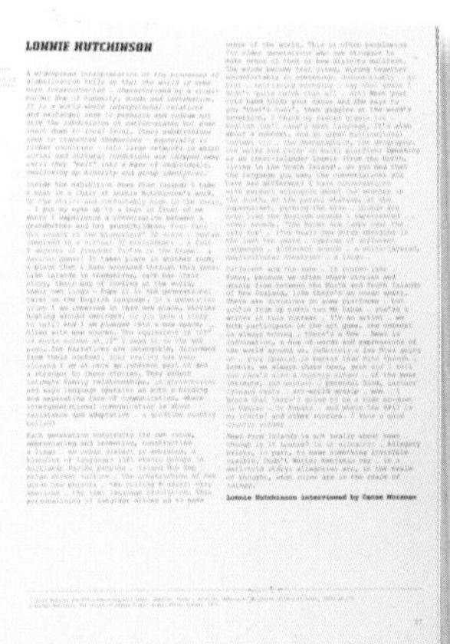

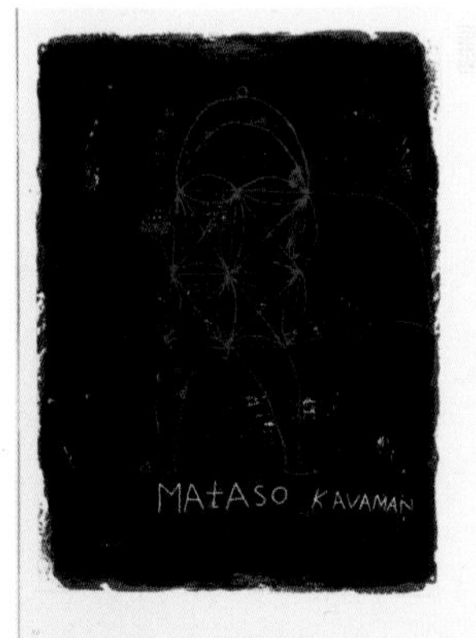

KIMIKO CHAN DESIGN | ART DIRECTOR **KIMIKO CHAN** | DESIGNER **KIMIKO CHAN** | CLIENT **ETUDE WINES**
PAPER/MATERIALS **MOHAWK SUPERFINE EGGSHELL COVER AND TEXT**

★ **Ó!** | ART DIRECTOR **MARIA ERICSDOTTIR** | DESIGNER **MARIA ERICSDOTTIR** | CLIENT **SAGA CAPITAL**

TIMBER DESIGN CO. INC | ART DIRECTOR **LARS LAWSON** | DESIGNER **LARS LAWSON** ★
CLIENT **HANCOCK REGIONAL HOSPITAL** | PAPER/MATERIALS **MOHAWK–BECKETT ENHANCE**

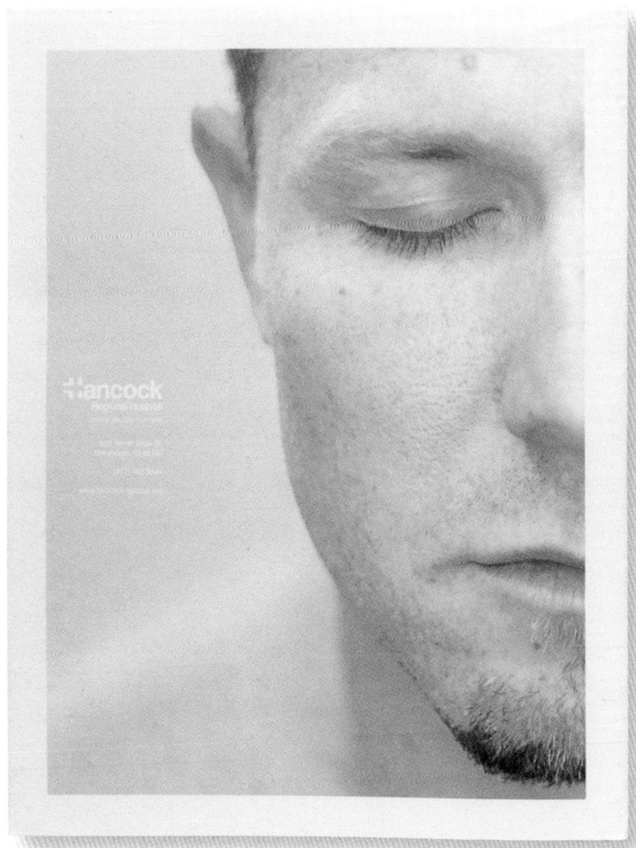

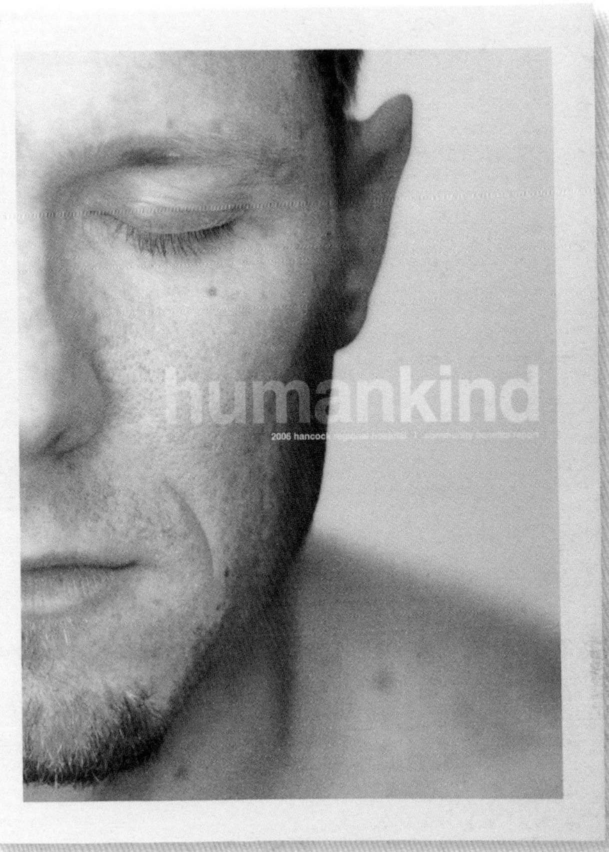

★ **SHINE ADVERTISING** | ART DIRECTOR **MICHAEL KRIEFSKI, JOHN KRULL** | DESIGNER **CHAD BOLLENBACH**
CLIENT **MADISON MALLARDS** | PAPER/MATERIALS **FINCH FINE VANILLA**

USA

⋆ COLD BEER ⋆

COMPENSATION

A Morale-Sapped Employee™, also known as an MSE, often feels under-appreciated, underpaid, and, of course, overworked (Fig. 3a). In response, many businesses prematurely resort to extreme measures to alleviate the problems at hand. These typically include: **A)** Giving an MSE a job title that indicates *"more responsibility,"* usually accomplished with the simple addition of the word "director" to an existing job title. **B)** Increasing an MSE's salary to accommodate the newly anointed "director" nomenclature. The good news? There exists a cheap and frosty alternative: beer. Cold beer. And yes, it flows free and unfettered at a Madison Mallards baseball game. With our help and expertise, that MSE in accounting will be a full-fledged BFE (Beer-Filled Employee™) by the top of the 3rd inning (Fig. 3b).

ENJOY THE BUDWEISER® SOLID ROCK ROOFTOP

(See p. 8) Employees having fun. Clients having fun. Mission accomplished. The Budweiser® Solid Rock Rooftop offers unlimited ballpark food, bottomless drinks, and a personal wait staff. For large groups, ask about renting the entire left field building, which includes the Budweiser® Solid Rock Rooftop and Outback Steakhouse Suites. ***Call 246-4277 today.***

4

(Fig. 3a) "My boss, Mr. Murray, is an idiot."

(Fig. 3b) "Well, hello there, Mr. Murray."

5

MADISON MALLARDS
ILLUSTRATED
⋆ GUIDE ⋆
To Employee
HAPPINESS & MORALE

MORALE. MOTIVATION. MALLARDS.

⋆ MOTIVATION ⋆

THROUGH HOT DOGS

Every year, thousands of businesses lose thousands of dollars due to low employee morale (Fig. 2a). We like to call it the High Cost of Low Morale Factor.™ The dilemma? How do you "fire up" a lethargic and despondent workforce without constantly threatening to fire them? Unfortunately, the answer isn't Hawaiian Shirt Friday,™ company picnic sack races, or putting together a Fun Committee.™ No, the solution is hot dogs. Good, old-fashioned American hot dogs. The kind that are plump and plentiful at every Madison Mallards baseball game. In fact, recent research indicates that workers who eat hot dogs are more productive and use fewer sick days than their non-hot-dog-eating counterparts (Fig. 2b). The bottom line: nothing puts a smile on an employee's face like a big, juicy wiener.

RESERVE THE OUTBACK STEAKHOUSE SUITES

(See p. 8) Motivate your workforce! Entertain your clients! The Outback Steakhouse Suites offer an exclusive private setting with your own personal wait staff. Enjoy ballpark food and a catered meal from the Outback Steakhouse with unlimited soda and beer. ***Call 246-4277 today.***

2

(Fig. 2a) "I hate my job."

(Fig. 2b) "Of course I can work this weekend!"

3

RIGSBY HULL | ART DIRECTOR **THOMAS HULL, LANA RIGSBY** | DESIGNER **THOMAS HULL** | CLIENT **WALTER P. MOORE** ★
PAPER/MATERIALS **MOHAWK SUPERFINE ULTIMATE WHITE**

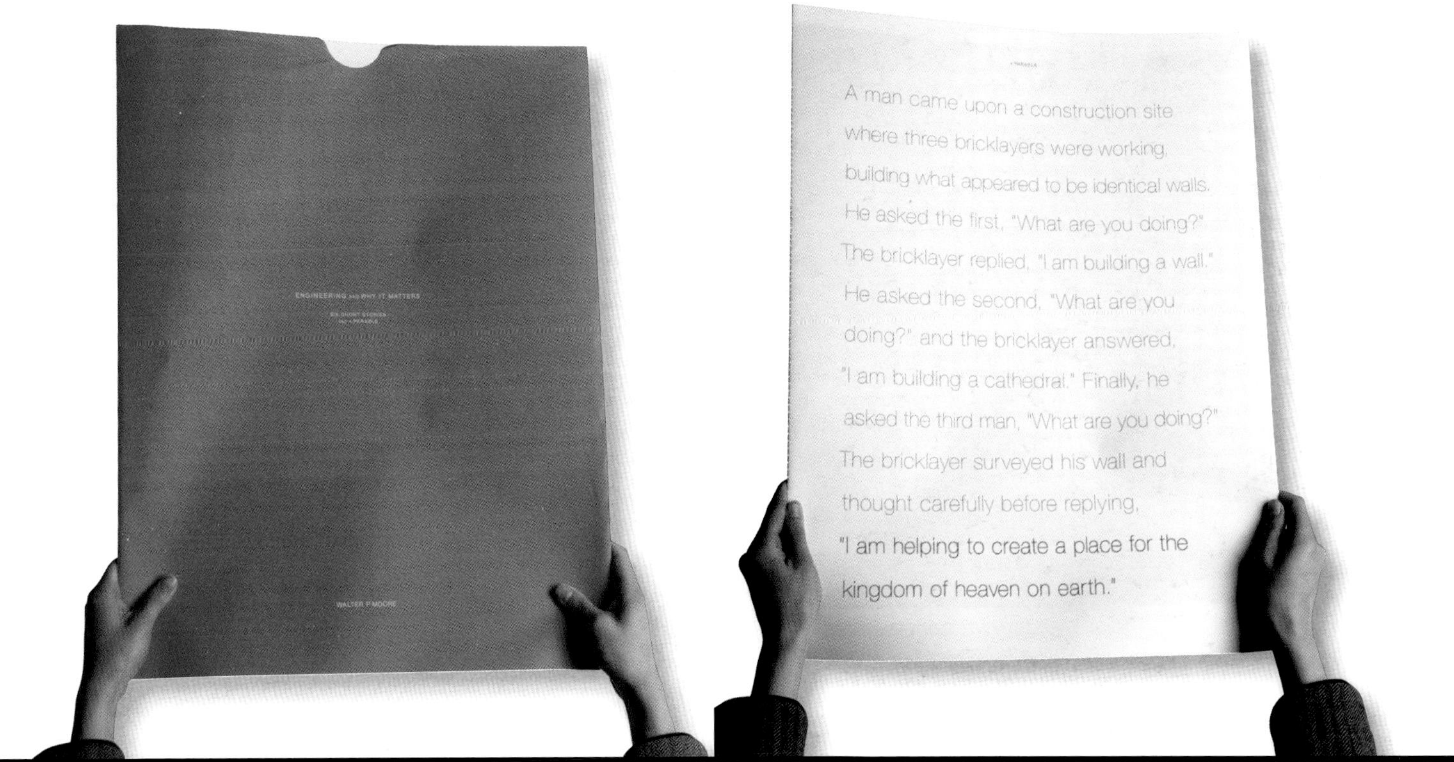

★ **RIGSBY HULL** | ART DIRECTOR **THOMAS HULL** | DESIGNER **THOMAS HULL, LANA RIGSBY** | CLIENT **WALTER P. MOORE**
PAPER/MATERIALS **MOHAWK SUPERFINE ULTIMATE WHITE**

NEO DESIGN | ART DIRECTOR **CRAIG HUTTON** | DESIGNER **CRAIG HUTTON** | CLIENT **PROSPERO** ★

UNITED KINGDOM

★ **NEO DESIGN** | ART DIRECTOR **CRAIG HUTTON** | DESIGNER **CRAIG HUTTON** | CLIENT **SHORT RICHARDSON + FORTH**

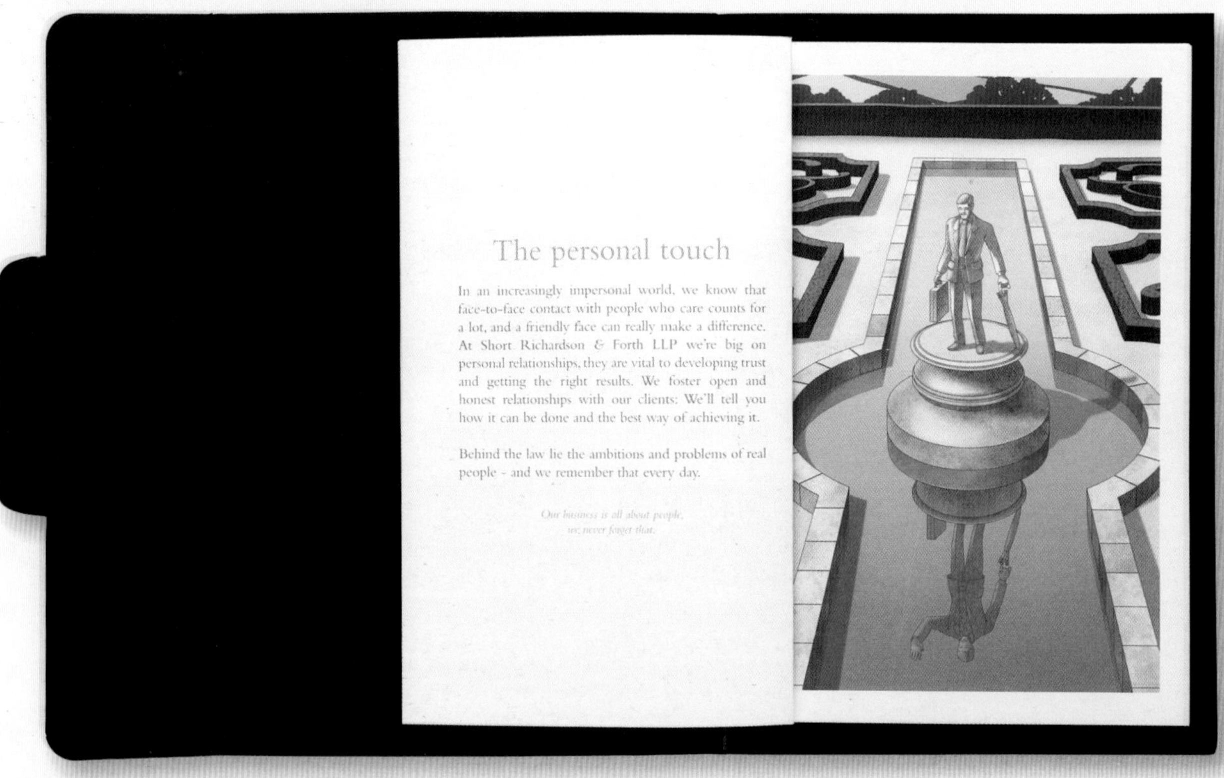

NEO DESIGN | ART DIRECTOR **CRAIG HUTTON** | DESIGNER **CRAIG HUTTON** | CLIENT **HOWIE WHITE RECRUITMENT** ★

★ **VOICE ADD PTE LTD** | ART DIRECTOR **JASON LEONG, ANDROS WONG** | DESIGNER **JERRY YAU**
CLIENT **MASONRY PTE LTD** | PAPER/MATERIALS **COVER AND TEXT: EXEL BULKY**

BLIK | ART DIRECTOR **TYLER BLIK** | DESIGNER **ANDREW GLENDINNING** | CLIENT **GREENWORKS STUDIO** ★
PAPER/MATERIALS **MOHAWK AND NEENAH ENVIRONMENT**

★ **SALTERBAXTER** | ART DIRECTOR **JAMES WILSON** | DESIGNER **STEWART CLARK, JENNIFER CHARON**
CLIENT **LAWRENCE GRAHAM** | PAPER/MATERIALS **MAGNO MATTE**

THE CHASE | ART DIRECTOR **STEPHEN ROYLE** | DESIGNER **STEPHEN ROYLE** ★

CLIENT **ROYAL COLLEGE OF PATHOLOGISTS** | PAPER/MATERIALS **NEENAH CLASSIC CREST AND CHIPBOARD**

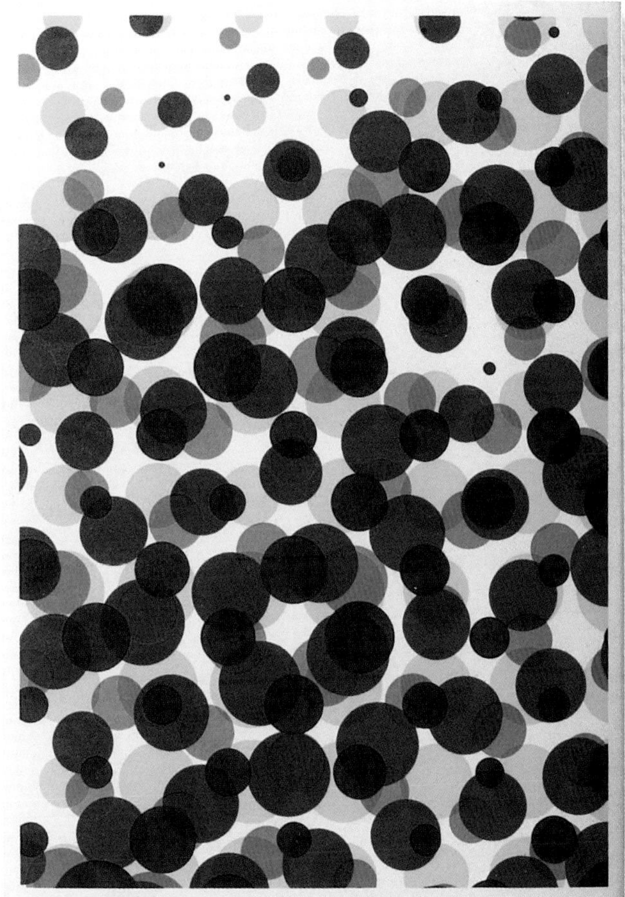

★ **SALTERBAXTER** | ART DIRECTOR **JAMES WILSON** | DESIGNER **CHRIS OATES, HANNAH GRIFFITHS, JENNIFER CHARON**
CLIENT **SALTERBAXTER** | PAPER/MATERIALS **THINK BRIGHT**

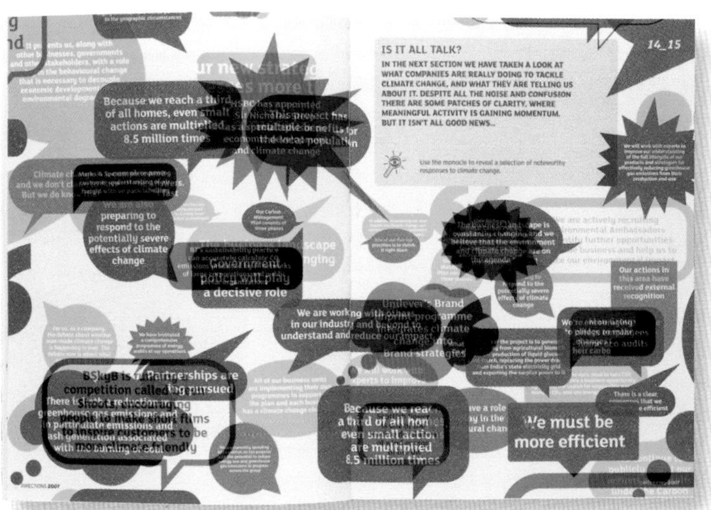

GREENWASH LIP-GLOSSING GREENWASH LIP-GLOSSING GREENWASH LIP-GLOSSING GREENWASH LIP-GLOSSING

SECRECY BRIBERY SECRECY BRIBERY SECRECY BRIBERY SECRECY BRIBERY

UNEMPLOYMENT ACCIDENT RATES UNEMPLOYMENT ACCIDENT RATES UNEMPLOYMENT ACCIDENT RATES UNEMPLOYMENT

SUPPLY CHAIN CHALLENGES CHILD LABOUR SUPPLY CHAIN CHALLENGES CHILD LABOUR SUPPLY CHAIN CHALLENGES CHILD LABOUR SUPPLY CHAIN CHALLENGES

SOCIAL EXCLUSION SKILLS GAP SOCIAL EXCLUSION SKILLS GAP SOCIAL EXCLUSION

CLIMATE CHANGE CLIMATE CHANGE

ONE WAY COMMUNICATION

BUSINESS

POINTS

TRUST REPUTATION GROWTH LICENCE TO OPERATE CONSUMER CONFIDENCE

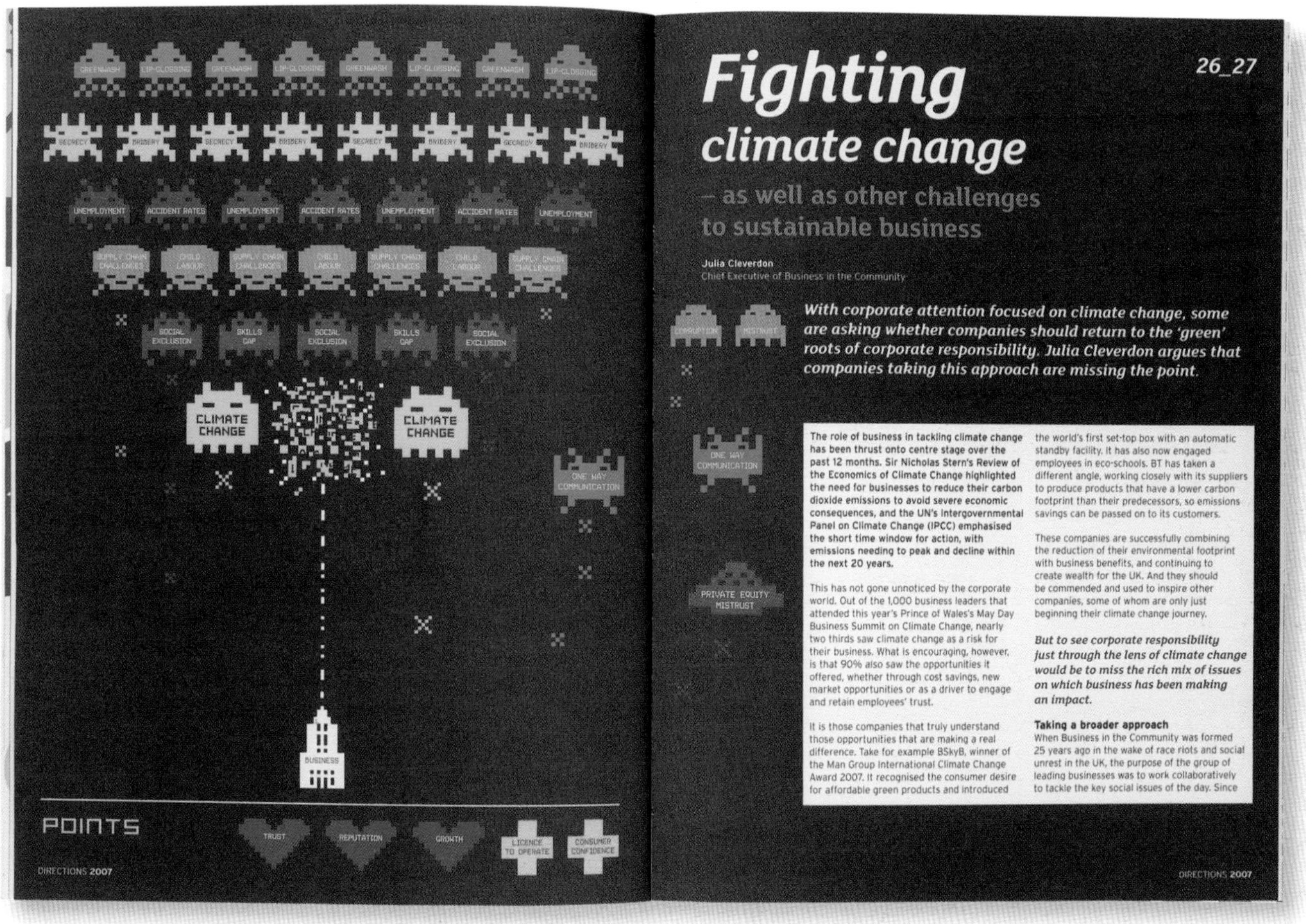

DIRECTIONS 2007

Fighting climate change

26_27

– as well as other challenges to sustainable business

Julia Cleverdon
Chief Executive of Business in the Community

CORRUPTION MISTRUST

With corporate attention focused on climate change, some are asking whether companies should return to the 'green' roots of corporate responsibility. Julia Cleverdon argues that companies taking this approach are missing the point.

ONE WAY COMMUNICATION

PRIVATE EQUITY MISTRUST

The role of business in tackling climate change has been thrust onto centre stage over the past 12 months. Sir Nicholas Stern's Review of the Economics of Climate Change highlighted the need for businesses to reduce their carbon dioxide emissions to avoid severe economic consequences, and the UN's Intergovernmental Panel on Climate Change (IPCC) emphasised the short time window for action, with emissions needing to peak and decline within the next 20 years.

This has not gone unnoticed by the corporate world. Out of the 1,000 business leaders that attended this year's Prince of Wales's May Day Business Summit on Climate Change, nearly two thirds saw climate change as a risk for their business. What is encouraging, however, is that 90% also saw the opportunities it offered, whether through cost savings, new market opportunities or as a driver to engage and retain employees' trust.

It is those companies that truly understand those opportunities that are making a real difference. Take for example BSkyB, winner of the Man Group International Climate Change Award 2007. It recognised the consumer desire for affordable green products and introduced the world's first set-top box with an automatic standby facility. It has also now engaged employees in eco-schools. BT has taken a different angle, working closely with its suppliers to produce products that have a lower carbon footprint than their predecessors, so emissions savings can be passed on to its customers.

These companies are successfully combining the reduction of their environmental footprint with business benefits, and continuing to create wealth for the UK. And they should be commended and used to inspire other companies, some of whom are only just beginning their climate change journey.

But to see corporate responsibility just through the lens of climate change would be to miss the rich mix of issues on which business has been making an impact.

Taking a broader approach
When Business in the Community was formed 25 years ago in the wake of race riots and social unrest in the UK, the purpose of the group of leading businesses was to work collaboratively to tackle the key social issues of the day. Since

DIRECTIONS 2007

UNITED KINGDOM

★ **SALTERBAXTER** | ART DIRECTOR **JAMES WILSON** | DESIGNER **HANNAH GRIFFITHS** | CLIENT **SALTERBAXTER**
PAPER/MATERIALS **THINK4 BRIGHT**

EBD | ART DIRECTOR **ELLEN BRUSS** | DESIGNER **GORDON CHISLETT** | CLIENT **WYNKOOP RESIDENCES** ★
PAPER/MATERIALS **NEENAH CLASSIC CREST AND CHIPBOARD**

★ IN THIS SECTION

URBANINFLUENCE

RETHINK

KARACTERS DESIGN GROUP

WALTERWAKEFIELD

DESIGN ARMY

WOW BRANDING

WILLOUGHBY DESIGN GROUP

THERE VISUAL COMMUNICATION DESIGN

ULHAS MOSES DESIGN STUDIO

SPRING ADVERTISING + DESIGN

CAMPBELL FISHER DESIGN

GDC–GUGLIELMINO DESIGN CO.

BRANDEX ADVERTISING, BRANDING + DESIGN

BURTON SNOWBOARDS/SYNDICATE

CREATIVE SPARK

DECKER DESIGN

HELENA SEO DESIGN

DESIGN RANCH

HANGAR 18 CREATIVE GROUP

BONBON LONDON

DEI CREATIVE

THE O GROUP

50,000 FEET INC.

ROYCROFT DESIGN

NOTHING: SOMETHING: NY

KORN DESIGN

PROPELLER

LISKA + ASSOCIATES

DESIGNBOLAGET

ELEVATOR

JKACZMAREK, FALLON

S DESIGN INC.

SK+G ADVERTISING

ENV DESIGN

FOLK CREATIVE MARKETING

BANDUJO ADVERTISING AND DESIGN

CHASE DESIGN GROUP, INC.

MILTON GLASER, INC.

WICKED CREATIVE

SAATCHI DESIGN

EBD

NEO DESIGN

JOHNSTON DUFFY

KOLEGRAM

CONNIE HWANG DESIGN

SHINE ADVERTISING

THE CHASE

DESIGN CENTER LTD.

PRODUCT AND SERVICE

★ **URBANINFLUENCE** | ART DIRECTOR **MIKE MATES, PETE WRIGHT** | DESIGNER **MIKE MATES, BRAD SHERMAN**
CLIENT **HILTON HOTELS**

URBANINFLUENCE | ART DIRECTOR **MIKE MATES, PETE WRIGHT** | DESIGNER **MIKE MATES** ★
CLIENT **QUEEN CITY GRILL**

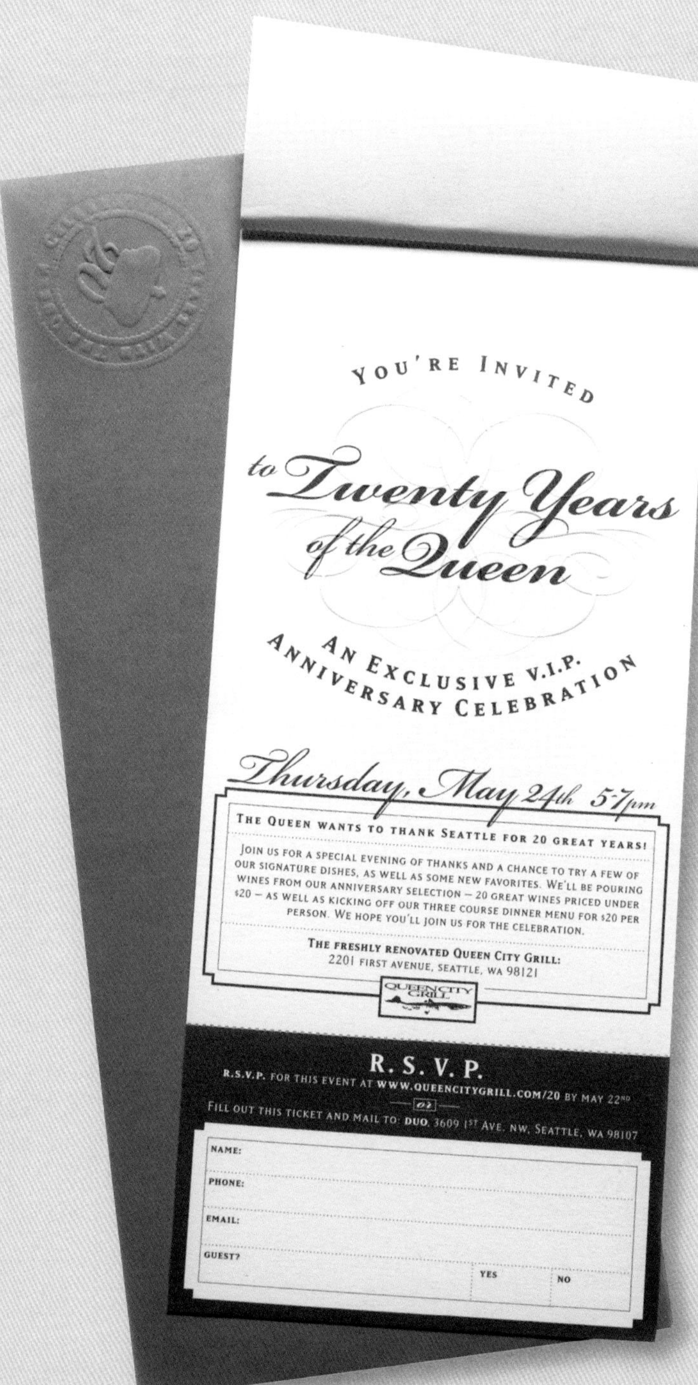

★ **RETHINK** | CREATIVE DIRECTOR **IAN GRAIS / CHRIS STAPLES** | DESIGNER **LISA NAKAMURA** | CLIENT **BARE**
PAPER/MATERIALS **COVER: 80 LB. PACESETTER MATTE COVER TEXT: 70 LB. PACESETTER TEXT WHITE**

CANADA

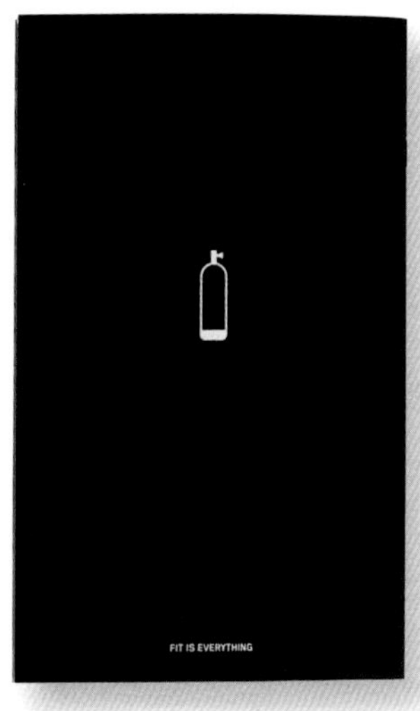

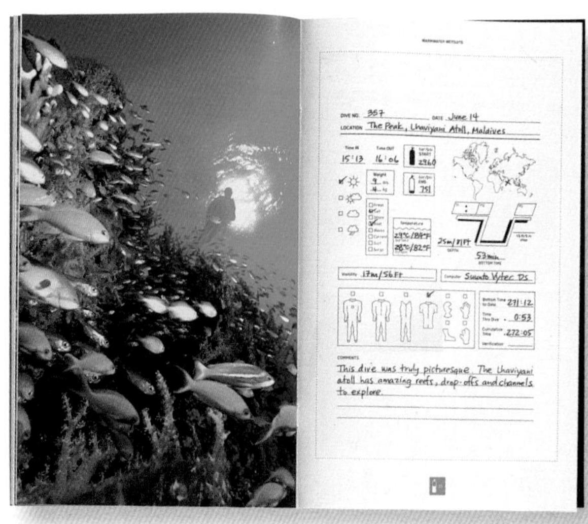

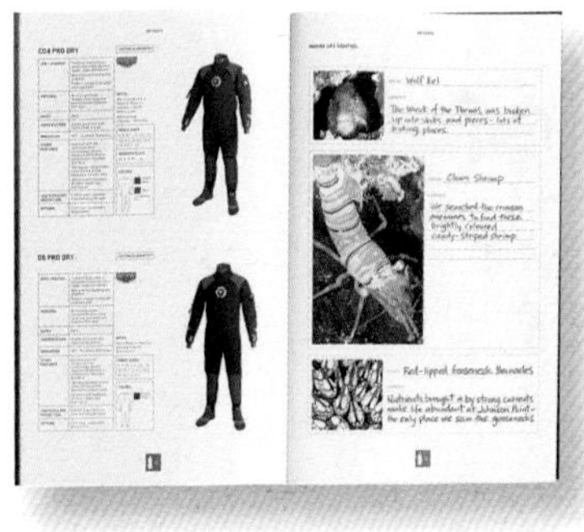

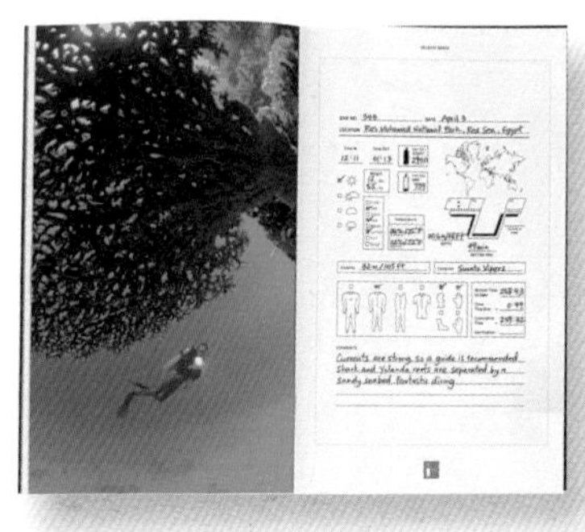

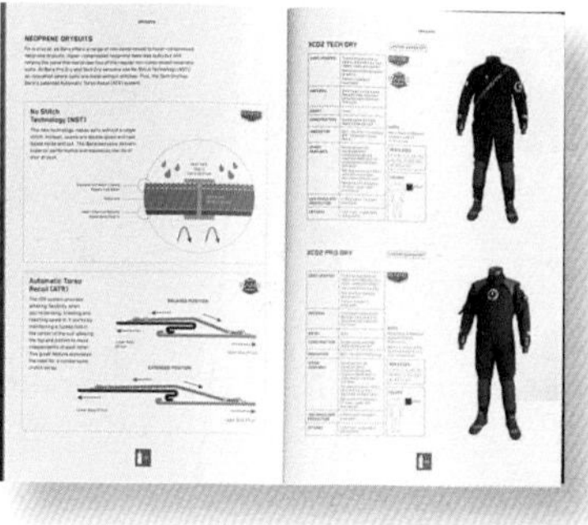

KARACTERS DESIGN GROUP | ART DIRECTOR **MARIA KENNEDY** | DESIGNER **TIM HOFFPAUIR** | CLIENT **VANOC** ★
PAPER/MATERIALS **MOHAWK OPTIONS, REICH PAPER CT. SOFT**

★ **WALTERWAKEFIELD** | ART DIRECTOR **JAIMY WALTER** | DESIGNER **PHOEBE BESLEY, MARIANNE MALAFOSSE, JAIMY WALTER**
CLIENT **SPICERS PAPER** | PAPER/MATERIALS **MONZA RECYCLED (VARIOUS) 130–400 GSM**

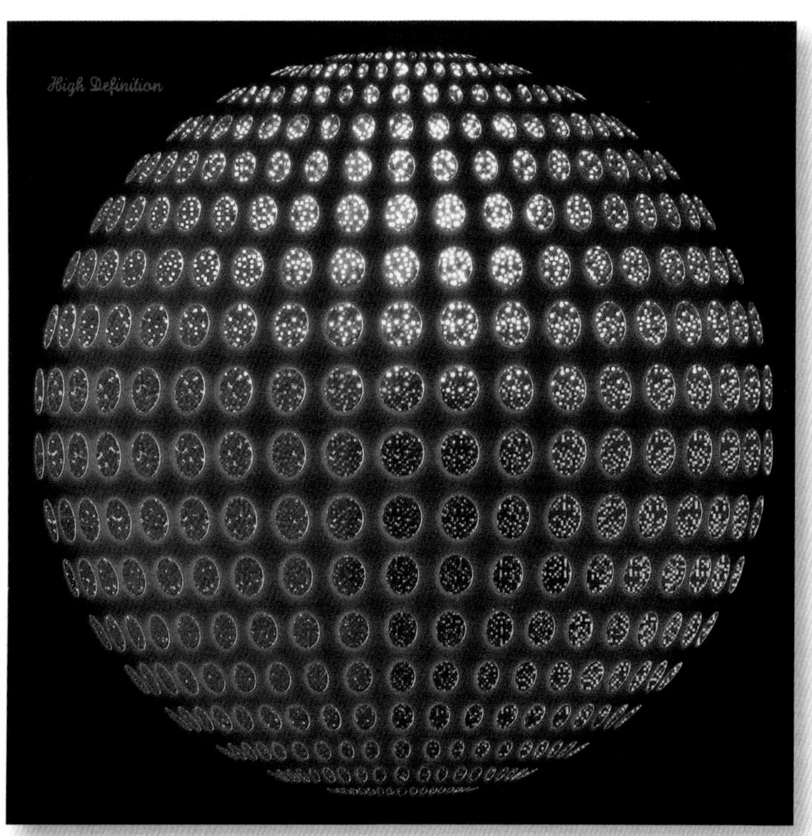

High Definition
GIMME
GIMME
GIMME
Madonna's single Hung Up features a sample of Abba's Gimme! Gimme! Gimme! (A Man After Midnight). The sample is a huge win for Madonna who became one of the rare artists to be endorsed by Abba to use one of their works as a sample.
Previously only The Fugees were granted this honor by Abba when they used a sample from The Name of the Game in their 1996 track Rumble in the Jungle. Benny and Bjorn from Abba broke their strict "no sample" rule on this occasion.
Hung Up was the first single from the album Confessions on a Dance Floor.
monza recycled
Mixed Sources
FSC

The album Living my Life begins with My Jamaican Guy, a reggae influenced mid-tempo track. Grace Jones wrote the song in Jamaican patois in parts, giving the track a quirky feel.
If you listen to it, you realise that L.L. Cool J sampled parts of this track in his song Doin' it. The album spawned three singles: My Jamaican Guy, Nipple to the Bottle and Everybody Hold Still.
monza recycled
Mixed Sources
FSC
Clarity
Feel Up

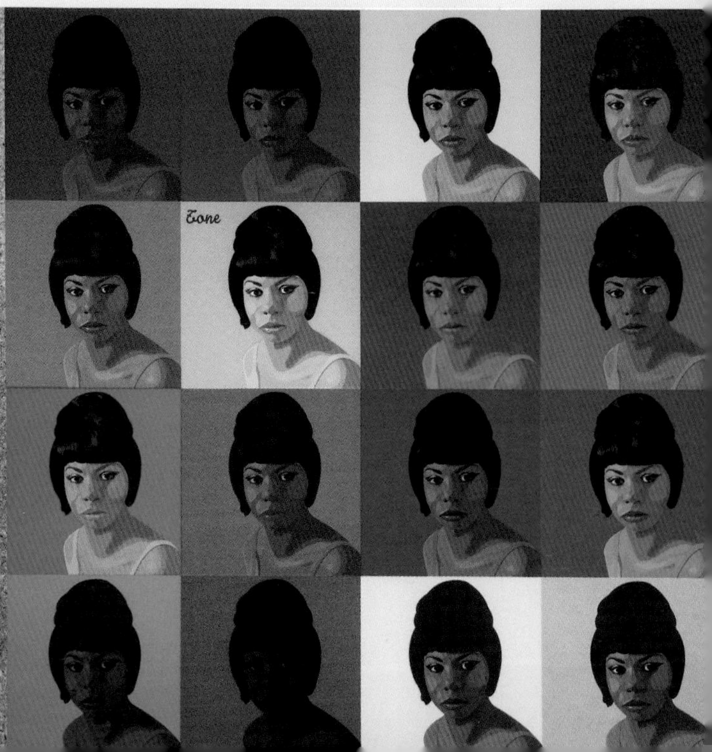

★ **DESIGN ARMY** | ART DIRECTOR **PUM LEFEBURE, JAKE LEFEBURE** | DESIGNER **TAYLOR BUCKHOLZ**
CLIENT **GOLDEN TRIANGLE BUSINESS IMPROVEMENT DISTRICT** | PAPER/MATERIALS **COUGAR, DIE CUT, GOLD FOIL STAMPING**

GOLDEN OPPORTUNITY

MEET YOUR NEIGHBORS

Live amongst the most stylish, glamorous and delicious neighbors in all of DC. A bustling, urban area filled with upscale names like The Hay Adams Hotel, Equinox Restaurant and BLT Steak, the Golden Triangle offers an ideal mix of big businesses, cool shops, fabulous restaurants and world-renowned salons. Not to mention, upscale hotels that average around $400/night. Just think, you could live next door to a trendy store known as Thomas Pink or one that's more classic like Brooks Brothers. Maybe you'd rather be closer to the Mayflower or one of the countless amazing restaurants. With an incredible $735 per square foot in sales among apparel retailers, this is your golden opportunity to be a part of one of the smartest neighborhoods in the city.

Imagine a place in the heart of Washington DC filled with highly successful urban professionals looking for convenient shopping. A place just steps away from the White House, K Street and upscale hotels where the most discriminating visitors stay. A luxurious place where DC powerhouses and travelers alike can stroll down a bustling, tree-lined street and find *Burberry* on their left, *Thomas Pink* on their right and a gem called the *Tiny Jewel Box* tucked in between. And when they've had their fill of high fashion, can stop for a delectable bite to eat at *The Palm* followed by a hair appointment at a trendy salon. Imagine a place that includes many major Metro stops and wealthy residential neighborhoods where a concert in the park can be heard in the summertime. A place like no other. Welcome to the Golden Triangle.

DESIGN ARMY | ART DIRECTOR **PUM LEFEBURE, JAKE LEFEBURE** | DESIGNER **PUM LEFEBURE** | CLIENT **RELISH**
PAPER/MATERIALS **FOX RIVER**

★

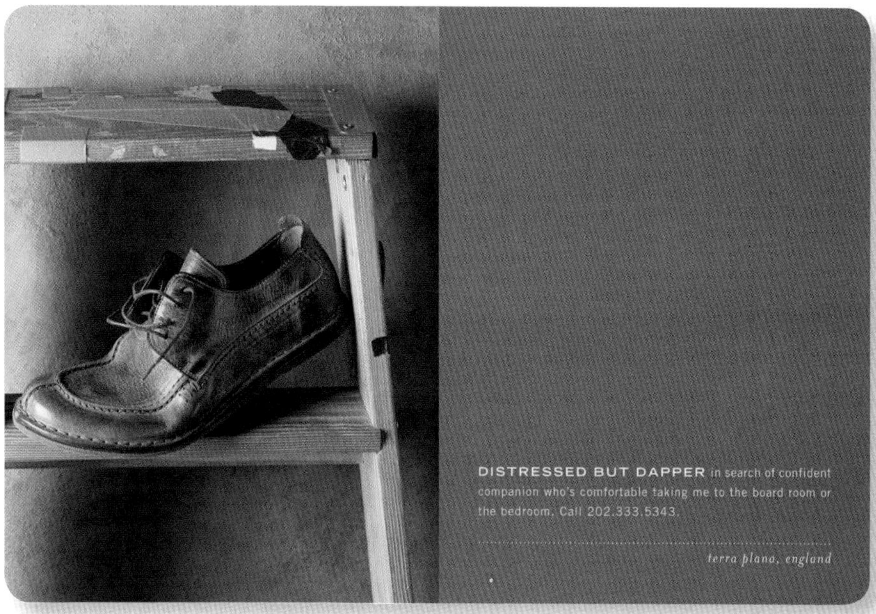

★ **WOW BRANDING** | DESIGNER **WILL JOHNSON, PERRY CHUA, JEFF SCHRAMM**
CLIENT **AVIVA SPORTS**

WILLOUGHBY DESIGN GROUP | ART DIRECTOR **ANN WILLOUGHBY, ZACK SHUBKAGEL** | DESIGNER **ZACK SHUBKAGEL** ★
CLIENT **SOUTHERN GRAPHICS COUNCIL**

★ **WILLOUGHBY DESIGN GROUP** | ART DIRECTOR **ANN WILLOUGHBY, NICOLE SATTERWHITE, DEB TAGTALIANIDIS**
DESIGNER **NICOLE SATTERWHITE, RYAN JONES, JESSICA MCENTIRE** | CLIENT **MOHAWK FINE PAPERS**
PAPER/MATERIALS **STRATHMORE WRITING AND SCRIPT**

WILLOUGHBY DESIGN GROUP | ART DIRECTOR **ANN WILLOUGHBY, ANNE SIMMONS** ★
DESIGNER **NATE HARDIN** | CLIENT **LINKS FITNESS**

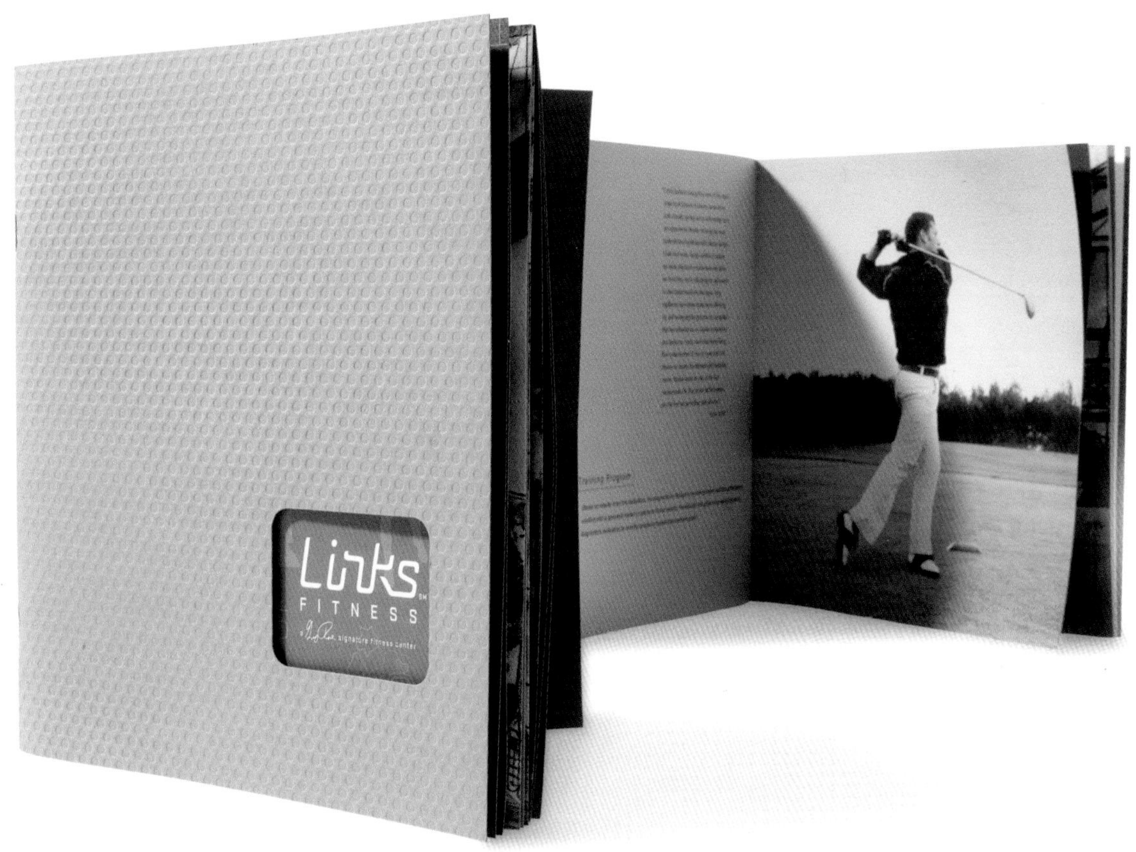

★ **THERE VISUAL COMMUNICATION DESIGN** | ART DIRECTOR **PAUL TABOURE** | DESIGNER **SIMON HANCOCK**
CLIENT **ORIENT EXPRESS HOTELS** | PAPER/MATERIALS **PREMIUM STOCK, MATTE CELLO, UV VARNISH, AND FOIL STAMPING**

ULHAS MOSES DESIGN STUDIO | ART DIRECTOR **ULHAS MOSES** | DESIGNER **ULHAS MOSES** | CLIENT **BRITISH COUNCIL**
PAPER/MATERIALS **GRUPPO NATURAL EVOLUTION IVORY**

★

★ **ULHAS MOSES DESIGN STUDIO** | ART DIRECTOR **ULHAS MOSES** | DESIGNER **ULHAS MOSES** | CLIENT **BRITISH COUNCIL**
PAPER/MATERIALS **GRUPPO NATURAL EVOLUTION IVORY**

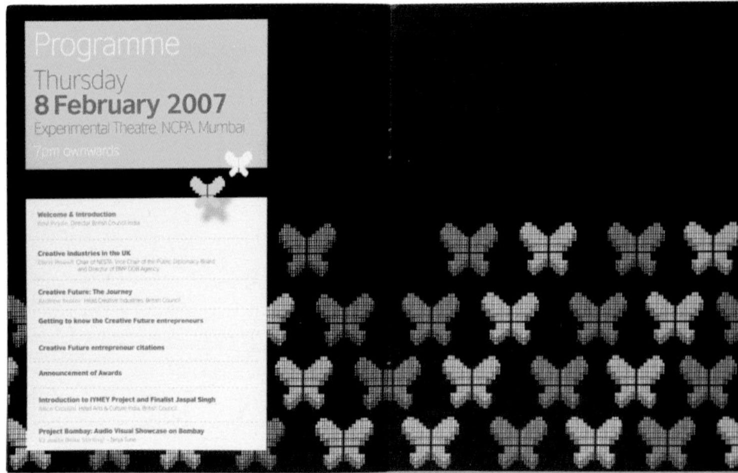

ULHAS MOSES DESIGN STUDIO | ART DIRECTOR **ULHAS MOSES** | DESIGNER **ULHAS MOSES** | CLIENT **UNLTD, UK** ★
PAPER/MATERIALS **MAP LITHO**

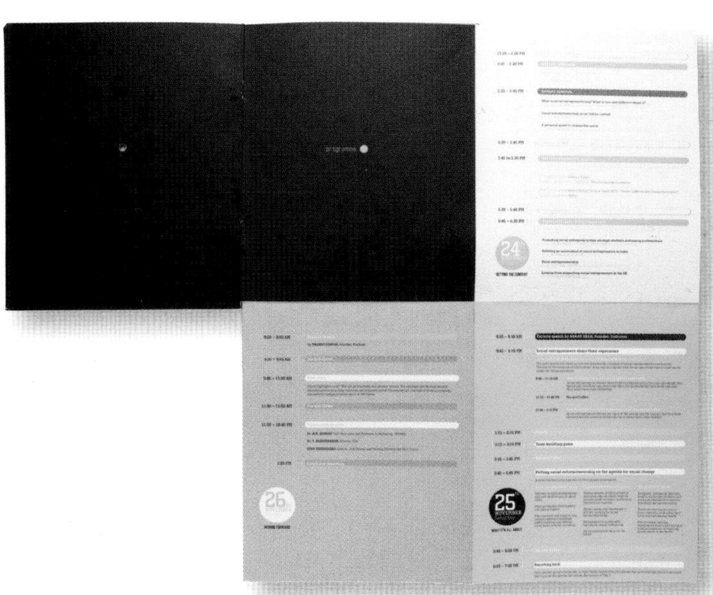

★ **SPRING ADVERTISING + DESIGN** | ART DIRECTOR **JAMES FILBRY, ROB SCHLYECHER** | DESIGNER **PERRY CHUA**
CLIENT **MAVERICK REAL ESTATE**

CAMPBELL FISHER DESIGN | ART DIRECTOR **GREG FISHER** | DESIGNER **GG LEMERE** | CLIENT **MARICOPA PARTNERSHIP FOR ARTS AND CULTURE** | PAPER/MATERIALS **DOMTAR SOLUTIONS CARRERA WHITE 65 LB. COVER** ★

USA

★ **GDC–GUGLIELMINO DESIGN CO.** | ART DIRECTOR **SID GUGLIELMINO** | DESIGNER **CHRIS DIXON**
CLIENT **ARTWORKERS ALLIANCE** | PAPER/MATERIALS **SOVEREIGN MATTE ART AND SOVEREIGN OFFSET**

Liana Kabel has a love affair with all things plastic. The plastic objects she uses as material are rich in their associations with the '1950s housewife' ideal and 'proper' feminine activities. However in Kabel's hands domesticity is thwarted and once functional objects are now loved not for their efficiency but for their vibrant colour and formal possibilities. Measuring tapes become flowers, knitting needles are transformed into bangles and Tupperware is melted to form abstract paintings to be worn as earrings or necklaces. Kabel's pieces encourage our attention to shift between the form and previous functions of these objects. The formal properties of colour, shape and line are as equally important as nostalgic qualities and domestic heritage, and this dualism allows Kabel's work to function on both aesthetic and personal levels.

By employing recycled objects from the domestic sphere, Kabel's jewellery speaks of times gone by and can evoke nostalgia for past moments that have been brought to life again through the encounter with a familiar object. As such, Kabel's works highlight the role second-hand objects can play as repositories of nostalgia, both real and created. Most of us are familiar with nostalgia as a feeling of longing and affective experience triggered by personal memories of the past. However, nostalgia can also be attached to objects and moments in time not experienced first-hand. In the latter, nostalgia is embodied in a stylised aesthetic that invokes socially constructed ideas of the past. These two concepts of nostalgia are conflated in Kabel's practice through the artist's use of recycled homewares which maintain connections to lived, everyday experience for many viewers, while simultaneously functioning on the level of retro, as fantastic plastic that embodies a culturally taught code of nostalgia.

SJ

1. **Knitwit rings**, 2007
Knitting needles
Courtesy of the artist

2. **Pastry flower earrings**, 2006
Plastic, rubber and sterling silver
Courtesy of the artist

3. **Tupperware Necklace**, 2006
Tupperware and sterling silver
Courtesy of the artist
Photo: Tim Nemeth
(Courtesy the Museum of Brisbane)

Liana Kabel

Liana Kabel was born in Sydney and is currently based in Brisbane, Australia. Since moving location Liana's artistic practice has seen a focus on the design and handcrafted production of contemporary jewellery.

Liana's background is broad ranging having also had experience in ceramics, photography, painting, fibre arts, costume design and the performing arts. Liana has completed a Bachelor of Arts from the University of New South Wales majoring in English and Theatre Studies.

Working as a full time artist, she divides her time between her home studio and her studio at Museum of Brisbane Workspace in City Hall.

"If it looks like a lolly, I like it"

Liana Kabel

50

BRANDEX ADVERTISING, BRANDING + DESIGN | ART DIRECTOR **TIM KELLY** | DESIGNER **KATE SIDI** ★
CLIENT **OPPENHEIMER** | PAPER/MATERIALS **MOHAWK SUPERFINE SMOOTH**

ORGANIC GROWTH
COMES NATURALLY

★ **BRANDEX ADVERTISING, BRANDING + DESIGN** | ART DIRECTOR **TIM KELLY** | DESIGNER **TIM KELLY**
CLIENT **OPPENHEIMER** | PAPER/MATERIALS **MOHAWK SUPERFINE SMOOTH**

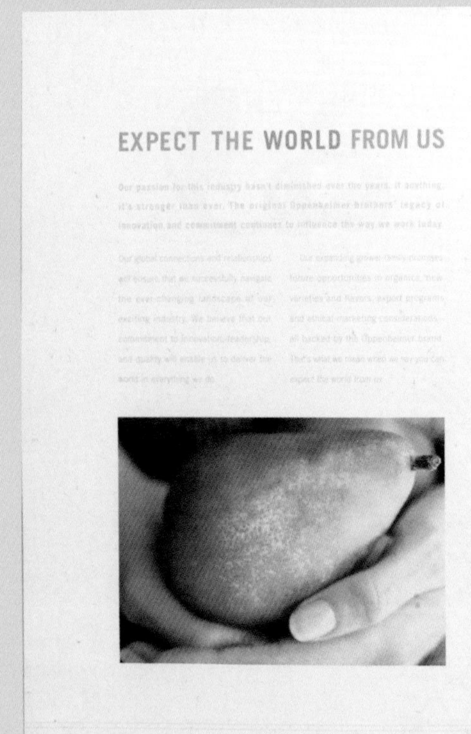

BRANDEX ADVERTISING, BRANDING + DESIGN | ART DIRECTOR **TIM KELLY** | DESIGNER **KATE SIDI** ★
CLIENT **ZESPRI KIWIFRUIT INTERNATIONAL** | PAPER/MATERIALS **MOHAWK SUPERFINE EGGSHELL**

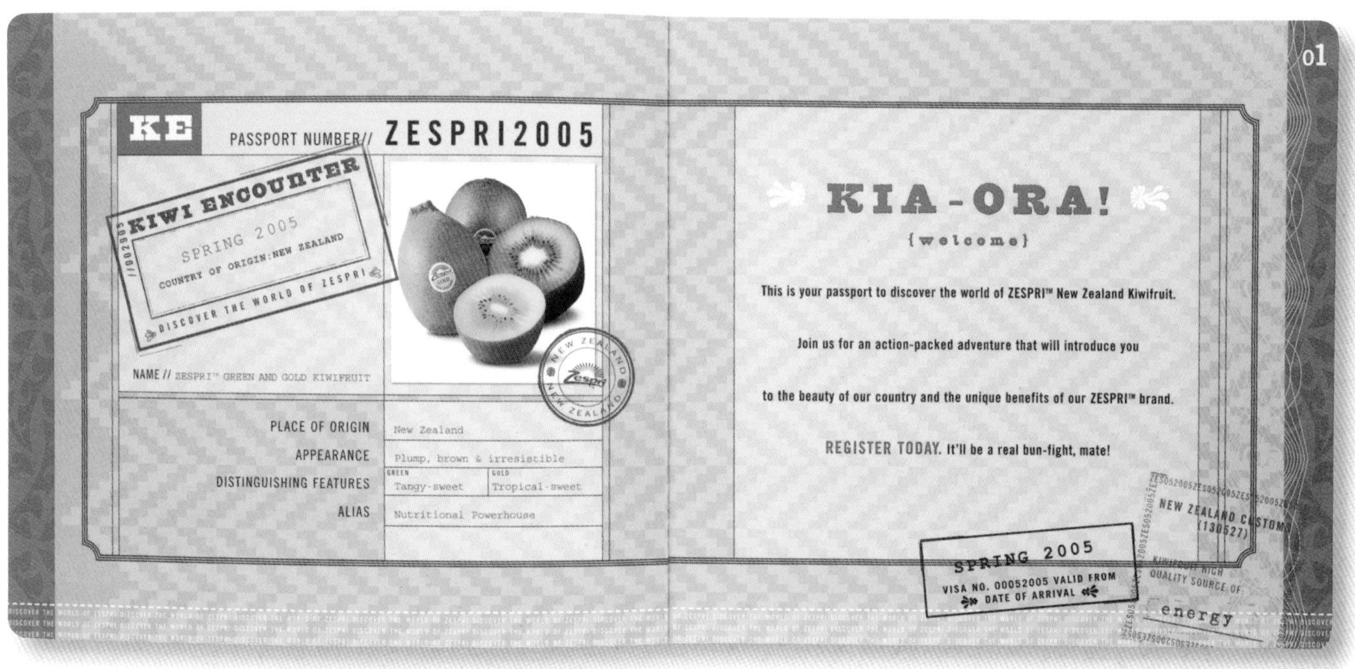

★ **BURTON SNOWBOARDS/SYNDICATE** | ART DIRECTOR **TOBY GRUBB** | DESIGNER **CRISTIN DENIGHT** | CLIENT **BURTON**

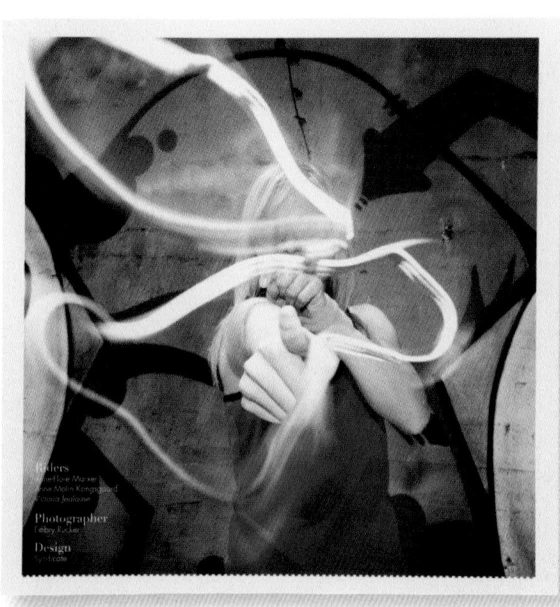

BURTON SNOWBOARDS/SYNDICATE | ART DIRECTOR **RICH CURREN** | DESIGNER **RICH CURREN, MIKE WOOD** ★
CLIENT **BURTON**

★ **BURTON SNOWBOARDS/SYNDICATE** | ART DIRECTOR **TOBY GRUBB** | DESIGNER **ADAM WEISS, DOUG CLARK, CRISTIN DENIGHT**
CLIENT **BURTON**

BURTON/SYNDICATE | ART DIRECTOR **ADAM WEISS** | DESIGNER **ADAM WEISS** | CLIENT **BURTON** ★

★ **BURTON/SYNDICATE** | ART DIRECTOR **ALEX LOWE** | DESIGNER **ADAM WEISS** | CLIENT **BURTON**

USA

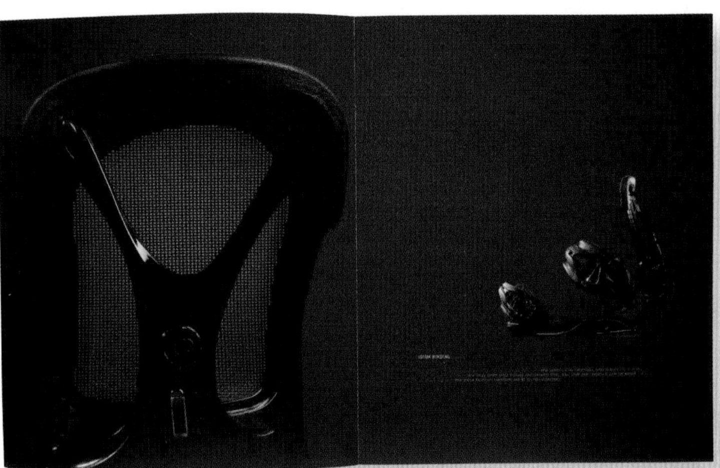

BURTON/SYNDICATE | ART DIRECTOR **ALEX LOWE** | DESIGNER **TOBY GRUBB, JOHN COSSEY, ALEX LOWE** ★
CLIENT **BURTON**

★ **BURTON/SYNDICATE** | ART DIRECTOR **ALEX LOWE** | DESIGNER **ADAM WEISS** | CLIENT **BURTON**

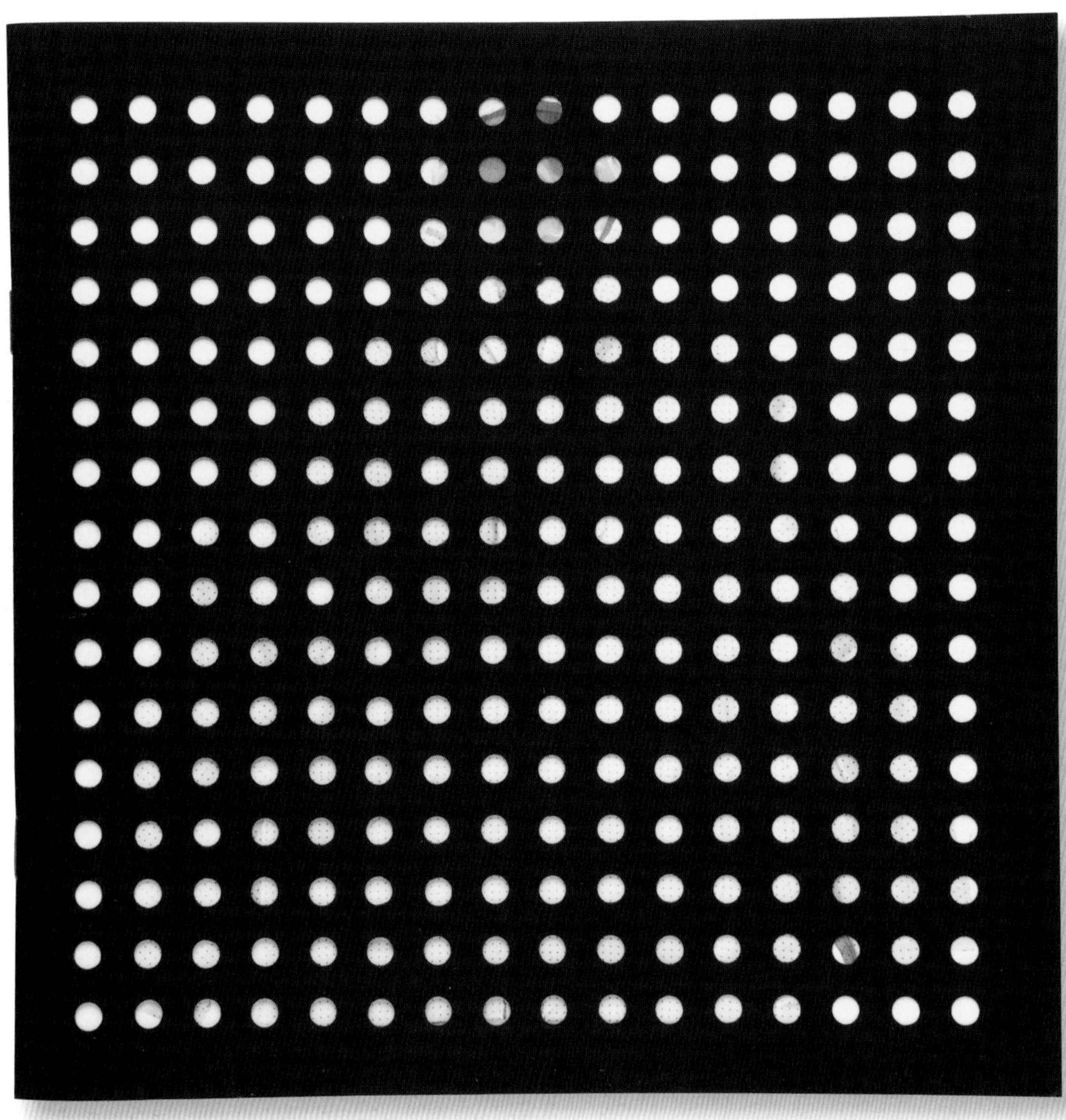

DESIGN RANCH | ART DIRECTOR/DESIGNER **MICHELLE SONDEREGGER, INGRED SIDIE** | CLIENT **BUCKLE** ★
PAPER/MATERIALS **CARDBOARD COVER WITH TAPE BINDING**

USA

★ **DESIGN RANCH** | ART DIRECTOR **MICHELLE SONDEREGGER, INGRED SIDIE** | DESIGNER **TAD CARPENTER, RACHEL KARACA, MICHELLE SONDEREGGER, INGRED SIDIE** | CLIENT **BUCKLE/LEE** | PAPER/MATERIALS **BOUND BOOK**

Jean is back. Dick is happy.
24
101Z | Limited Edition | 394-1441 | Real Dry
For more information or product samples contact
Angela Sciara 816.512.9160 or Jennifer Johnson 913.789.0705.

Jane considers a performance art piece involving Jean.
Jean likes performance art. Jean thinks performance art is tops.
16
17

This is Jean.
This is Dick.
2
3

This is Jean.
2

This is Jane.
3

★ **DESIGN RANCH** | ART DIRECTOR **MICHELLE SONDEREGGER, INGRED SIDIE** | DESIGNER **BRYNN JOHNSON**
CLIENT **LEE** | PAPER/MATERIALS **HARD BOUND, ACCORDION-FOLD BOOK**

DESIGN RANCH | ART DIRECTOR **MICHELLE SONDEREGGER, INGRED SIDIE** ★
DESIGNER **TAD CARPENTER, BRYNN JOHNSON** | CLIENT **LEE**

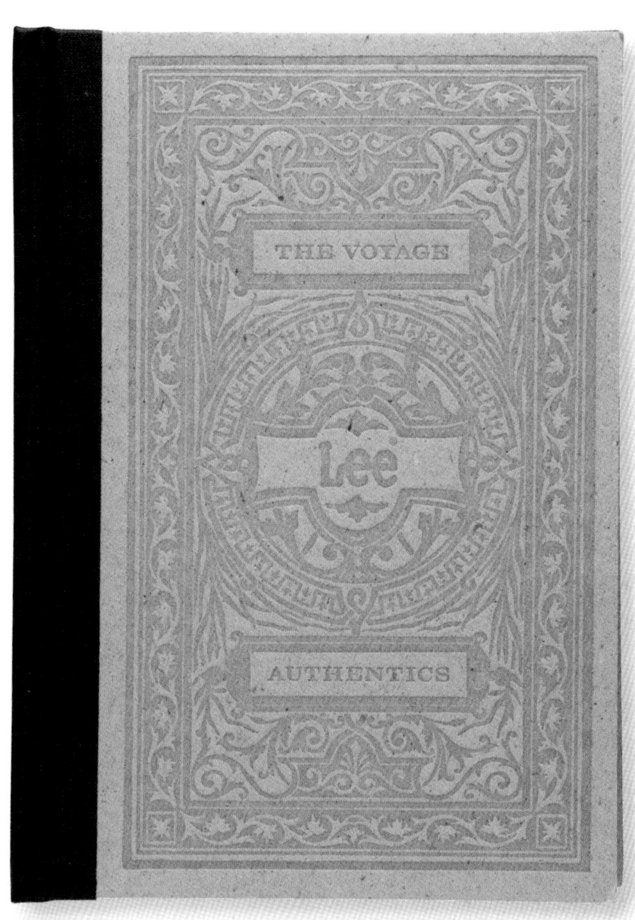

★ **HELENA SEO DESIGN** | ART DIRECTOR **HELENA SEO** | DESIGNER **HELENA SEO** | CLIENT **INEKE, LLC**
PAPER/MATERIALS **COVER: NEENAH ULTRA UV II, 28 LB., TEXT: MOHAWK SUPERFINE 100 LB.**

USA

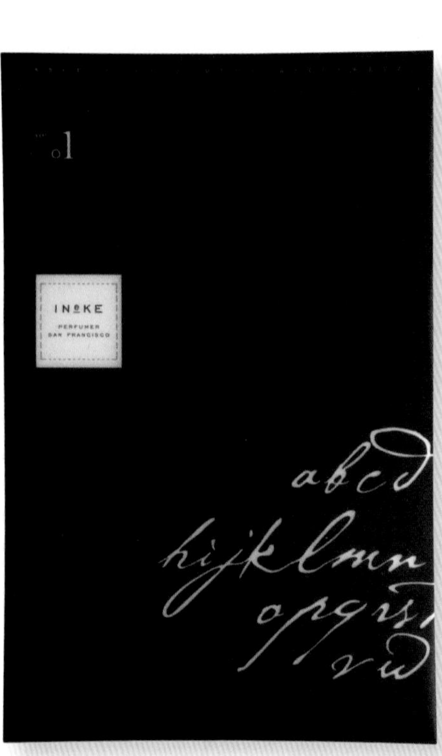

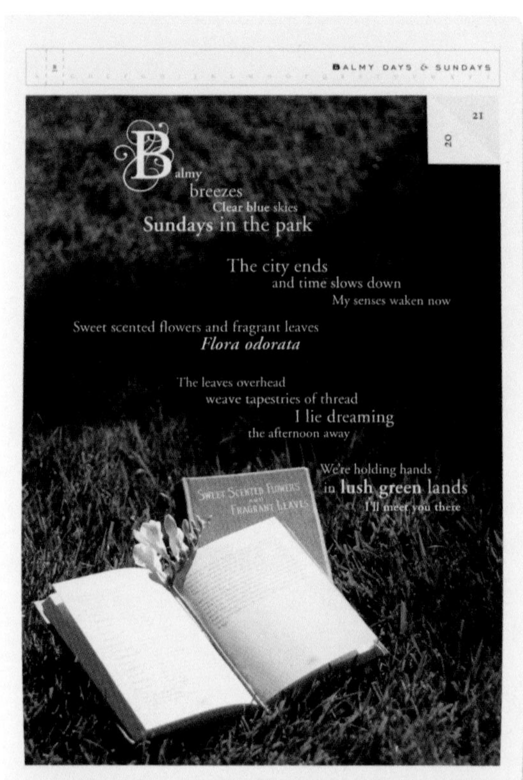

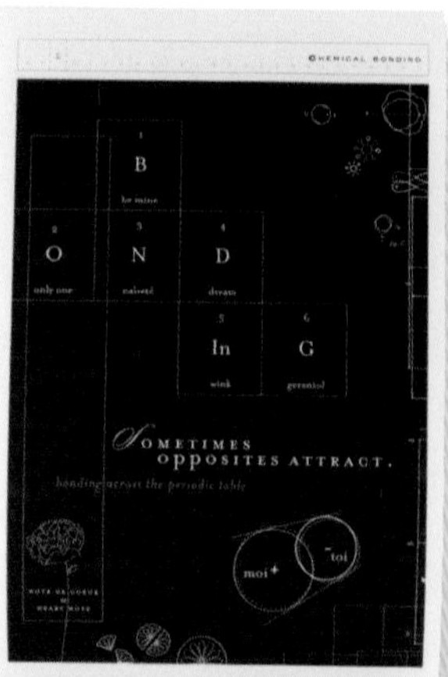

DESIGN RANCH | ART DIRECTOR **MICHELLE SONDEREGGER, INGRED SIDIE** | DESIGNER **BRYNN JOHNSON** ★
CLIENT **LEE** | PAPER/MATERIALS **ACCORDION-FOLD BOOK**

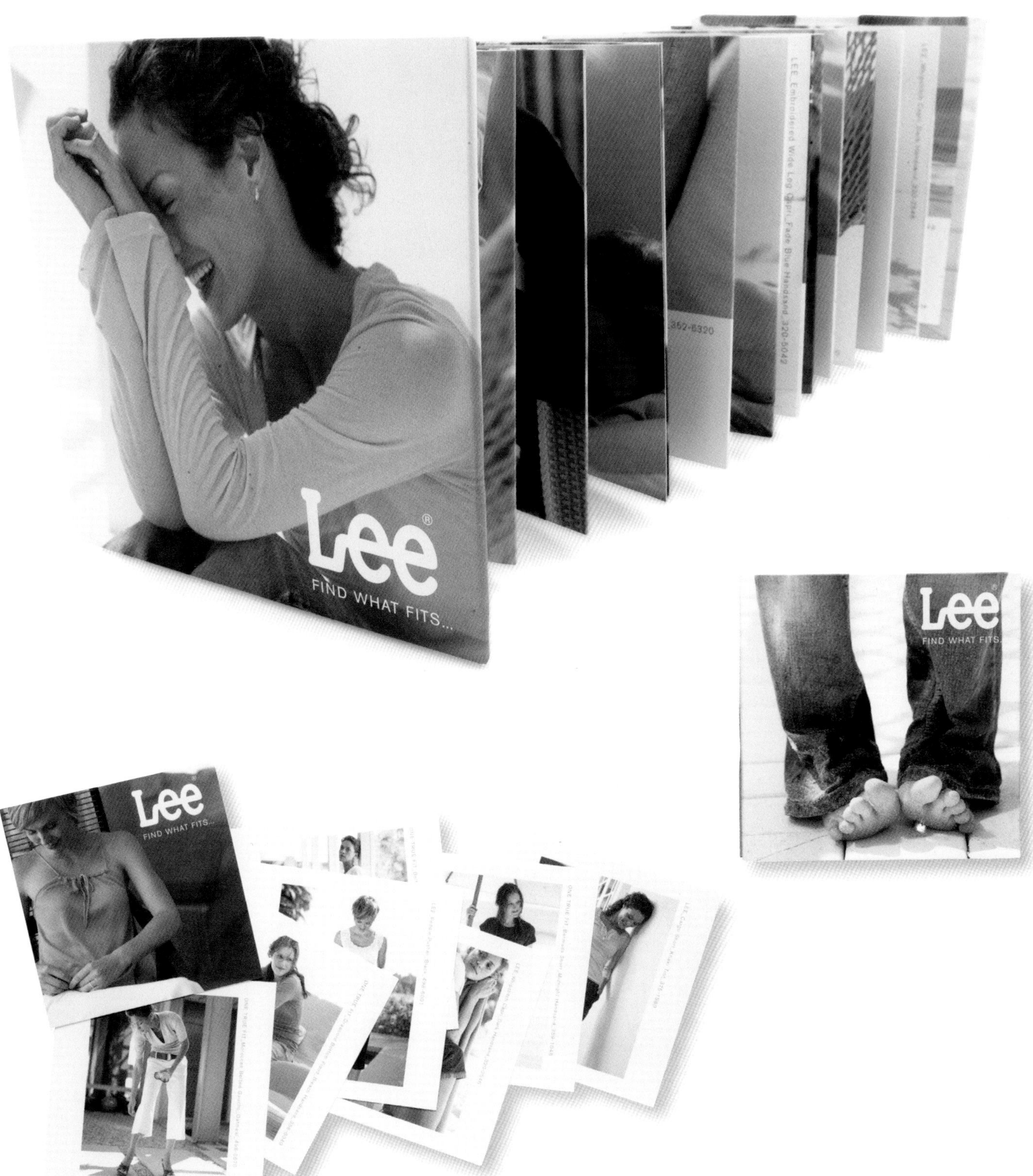

★ **DESIGN RANCH** | ART DIRECTOR **MICHELLE SONDEREGGER, INGRED SIDIE** | DESIGNER **TAD CARPENTER**
CLIENT **RAETA ESTATES** | PAPER/MATERIALS **LETTERPRESSED CARDBOARD AND FRENCH PAPER**

USA

DESIGN RANCH | ART DIRECTOR **MICHELLE SONDEREGGER, INGRED SIDIE** | DESIGNER **MICHELLE MARTYNOWICZ, TAD CARPENTER** ★
CLIENT **BUCKLE** | PAPER/MATERIALS **NEWSPRINT**

★ **HANGAR 18 CREATIVE GROUP** | ART DIRECTOR **SEAN CARTER** | DESIGNER **SEAN CARTER** | CLIENT **UNISOURCE**

BONBON LONDON | ART DIRECTOR **MARK HARPER, SASHA CASTLING** | DESIGNER **MARK HARPER**
CLIENT **DANIEL COBB** | PAPER/MATERIALS **NATURALIS SMOOTH RECYCLED 160 GSM AND BEDROCK**

★ **DEI CREATIVE** | ART DIRECTOR **SARA GREEN, SHANNON PALMER** | DESIGNER **NOAH BELL**
CLIENT **EK REAL ESTATE + TRACE LOFTS, LLC.** | PAPER/MATERIALS **MOHAWK OPTIONS, THREAD**

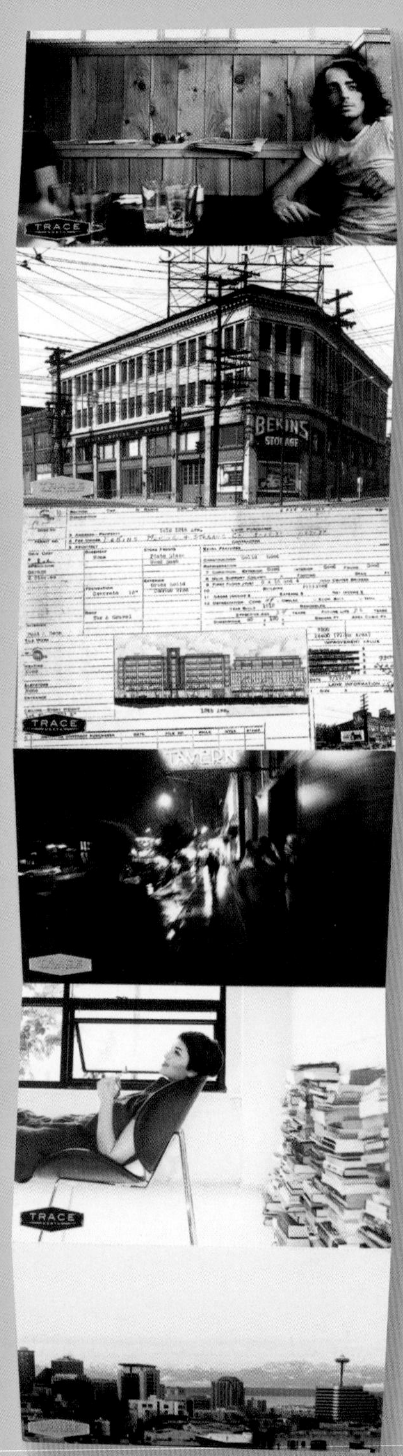

THE O GROUP | ART DIRECTOR **JASON B. COHEN, KARIN SATROM** | DESIGNER **MARITES ALGONES, TANYA POPADICS, ALEX AMMAR** ★
CLIENT **MÖET HENNESSY USA** | PAPER/MATERIALS **UTOPIA U1X SILK 80 LB. COVER, GOLD FOIL EMBOSSED STICKER**

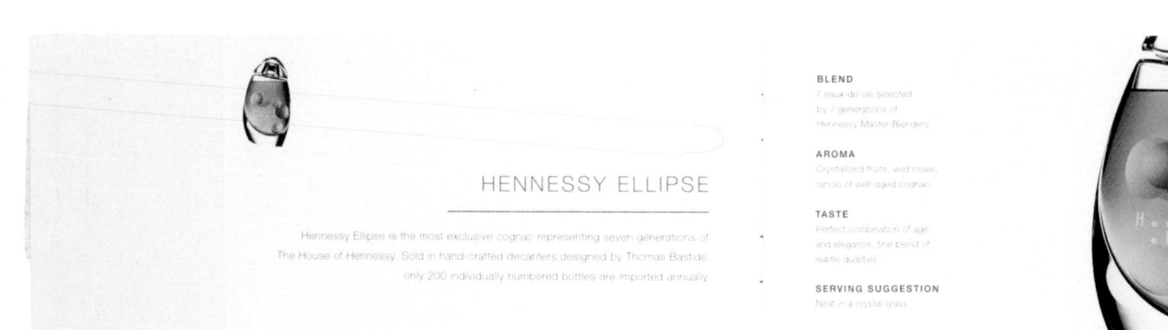

HENNESSY V.S WORLD COCKTAILS

HENNESSY NEW YORK

HENNESSY HAVANA

HENNESSY SHANGHAI

HENNESSY PARIS

★ **THE O GROUP** | ART DIRECTOR **JASON B. COHEN, J. KENNETH ROTHERMICH** | DESIGNER **J. KENNETH ROTHERMICH**
CLIENT **NORTH DEVELOPMENT GROUP** | PAPER/MATERIALS **MOHAWK ULTRAWHITE SMOOTH 100 LB. COVER, 100 LB. TEXT AND 80 LB. TEXT**

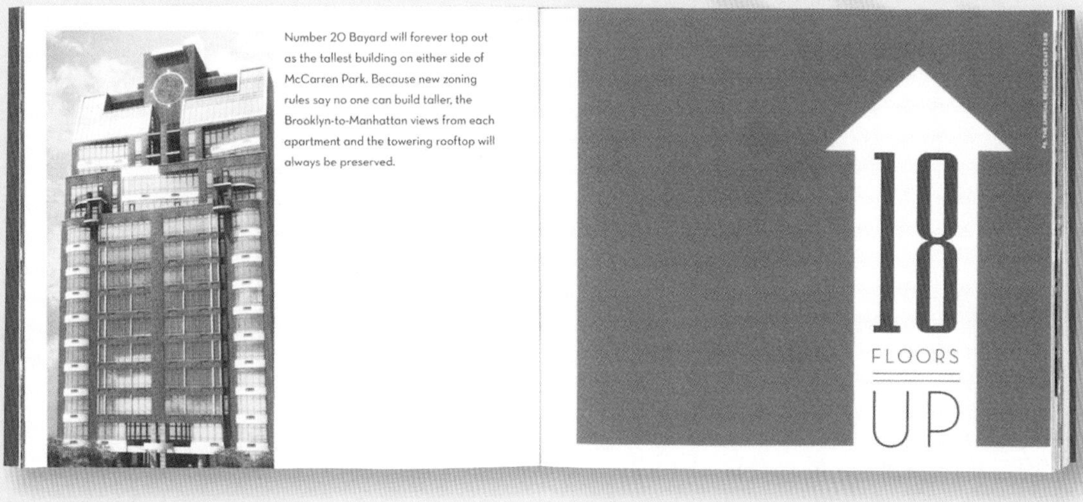

Number 20 Bayard will forever top out as the tallest building on either side of McCarren Park. Because new zoning rules say no one can build taller, the Brooklyn-to-Manhattan views from each apartment and the towering rooftop will always be preserved.

★ **50,000 FEET INC.** | ART DIRECTOR **TRACY WEST** | DESIGNER **TRACY WEST, JOHNNY MEI**
CLIENT **MINI/BMW OF NORTH AMERICA, LLC.** | PAPER/MATERIALS **SAPPI LUSTRO GLOSS 100 LB. COVER**

USA

RALLY INTERNATIONAL ICON

MINI MOTORINGGEAR FALL/WINTER 2007

Most stories follow a time-honored formula: beginning, middle and end. But in the world of MINI, things work a little differently. For instance, you might start out in one direction only to veer off in another. Or discover that an end is really a beginning in disguise. In that spirit, we're proud to present a trio of new collections from MINI MotoringGear, engineered for spinning on- and off-road tales in inimitable MINI style. **RALLY COLLECTION** A race-inspired throwback to a time when MINI reigned supreme in Monte Carlo and the world was put on notice. **INTERNATIONAL COLLECTION** Eye-grabbing designs drawn from an ever-growing MINI nation that stretches across countries and continents alike. **ICON COLLECTION** Classic colors and timeless lines converge in a look that's pure, unadulterated MINI. Outfitted with this introduction, you're ready to write your own chapter in motoring history. We trust that, as with any great road, it'll have more than enough twists and turns to keep things interesting.

EVERY STORY HAS TO START SOMEWHERE.

50,000 FEET INC. | ART DIRECTOR **TRACY WEST** | DESIGNER **JOHNNY MEI, TRACY WEST** ★
CLIENT **MINI/BMW OF NORTH AMERICA, LLC.** | PAPER/MATERIALS **SAPPI OPUS**

★ **50,000 FEET INC.** | ART DIRECTOR **MICHAEL PETERSEN** | DESIGNER **MICHAEL PETERSEN** | CLIENT **TERLATO WINES**
PAPER/MATERIALS **MOHAWK SUPERFINE ULTRAWHITE**

TWO HANDS WINES
GARDEN SERIES EXPERIENCE
TASTING GUIDE

OUR MISSION:
TO SHOWCASE THE DIVERSITY OF AUSTRALIAN SHIRAZ BY HIGHLIGHTING THE REGIONAL CHARACTERISTICS AND ALLOWING THE FRUIT TO BE THE PRIMARY FEATURE OF THE WINE.
Two Hands
2005 Max's Garden Heathcote Shiraz
Two Hands
2005 Sophie's Garden Padthaway Shiraz
Two Hands
Two Hands
2005 Bella's Garden Barossa Valley Shiraz
MICHAEL TWELFTREE
RICHARD MINTZ

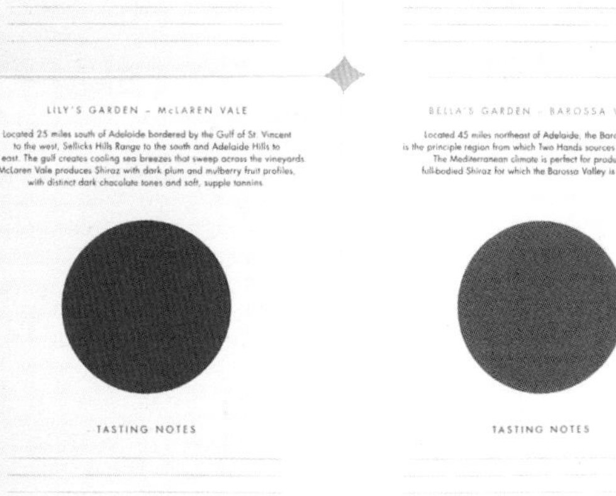
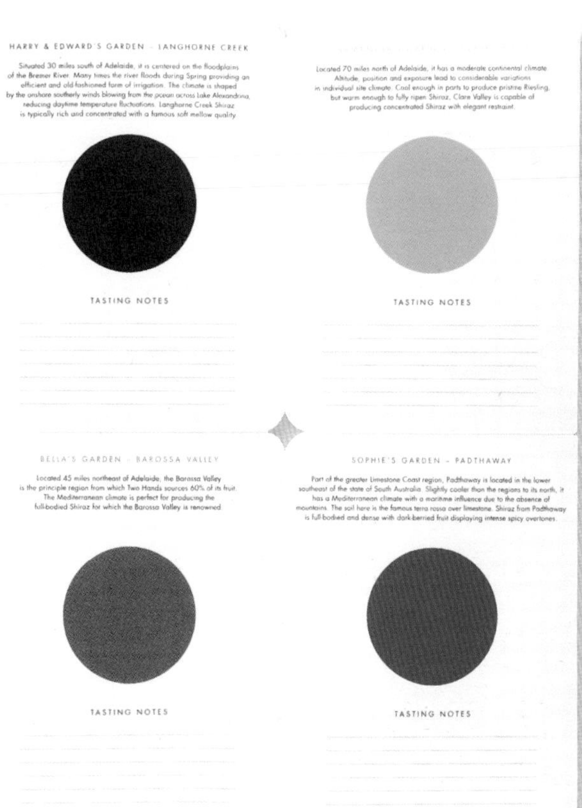
MAX'S GARDEN – HEATHCOTE
Located 75 miles north of Melbourne in Central Victoria, the climate and soils are strongly influenced by the Mount Camel Range, which provides a natural tunneling for the prevailing cool south to southeast winds. The secret here is the oldest soil in Australia, deep red Cambrian pulverized rock that is 500 million years old. Heathcote produces world-class Shiraz with distinctive character, depth and richness.
TASTING NOTES
HARRY & EDWARD'S GARDEN – LANGHORNE CREEK
Situated 30 miles south of Adelaide, it is centered on the floodplains of the Bremer River. Many times the river floods during Spring providing an efficient and old-fashioned form of irrigation. The climate is shaped by the onshore southerly winds blowing from the ocean across Lake Alexandrina, reducing daytime temperature fluctuations. Langhorne Creek Shiraz is typically rich and concentrated with a famous soft mellow quality.
TASTING NOTES
Located 70 miles north of Adelaide, it has a moderate continental climate. Altitude, position and exposure lead to considerable variations in individual site climate. Cool enough in parts to produce pristine Riesling, but warm enough to fully ripen Shiraz, Clare Valley is capable of producing concentrated Shiraz with elegant restraint.
TASTING NOTES
LILY'S GARDEN – McLAREN VALE
Located 25 miles south of Adelaide bordered by the Gulf of St. Vincent to the west, Sellicks Hills Range to the south and Adelaide Hills to the east. The gulf creates cooling sea breezes that sweep across the vineyards. McLaren Vale produces Shiraz with dark plum and mulberry fruit profiles, with distinct dark chocolate tones and soft, supple tannins.
TASTING NOTES
BELLA'S GARDEN – BAROSSA VALLEY
Located 45 miles northeast of Adelaide, the Barossa Valley is the principle region from which Two Hands sources 60% of its fruit. The Mediterranean climate is perfect for producing the full-bodied Shiraz for which the Barossa Valley is renowned.
TASTING NOTES
SOPHIE'S GARDEN – PADTHAWAY
Part of the greater Limestone Coast region, Padthaway is located in the lower southeast of the state of South Australia. Slightly cooler than the regions to its north, it has a Mediterranean climate with a maritime influence due to the absence of mountains. The soil here is the famous terra rossa over limestone. Shiraz from Padthaway is full-bodied and dense with dark-berried fruit displaying intense spicy overtones.
TASTING NOTES

★ **50,000 FEET INC.** | ART DIRECTOR **KEN FOX, TRACY WEST** | DESIGNER **TRACY WEST, ADAM DINES**
CLIENT **TERLATO WINES** | PAPER/MATERIALS **MOHAWK SUPERFINE ULTRAWHITE, SIERRA BOOK CLOTH**

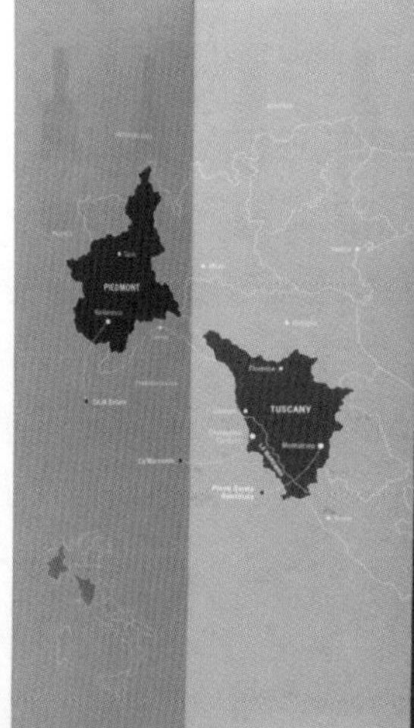

GAJA
1859

★ **50,000 FEET INC.** | ART DIRECTOR **KEN FOX, JIM MISENER** | DESIGNER **TRACY WEST** | CLIENT **TERLATO WINES**
PAPER/MATERIALS **MOHAWK SUPERFINE ULTRAWHITE**

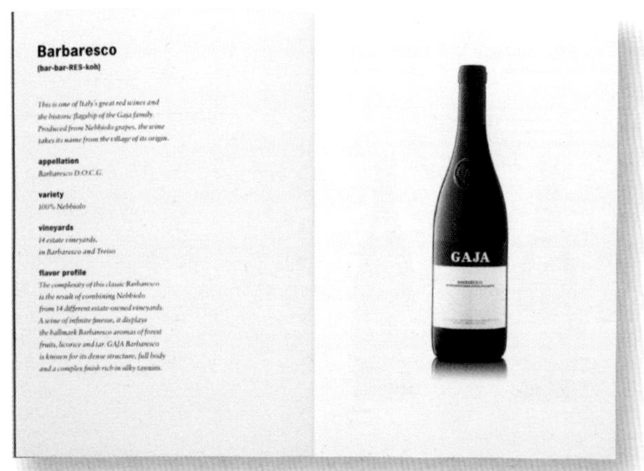

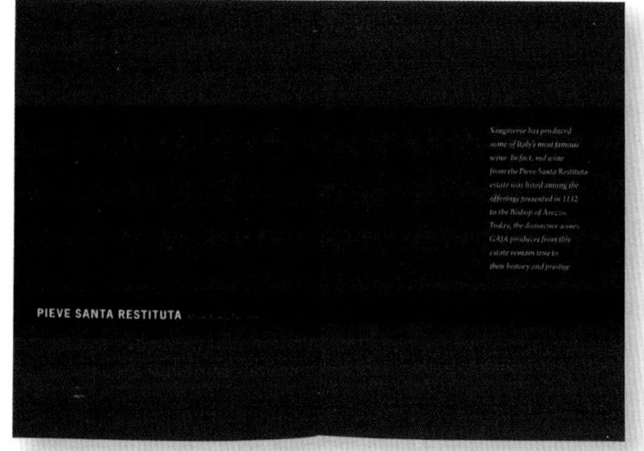

NOTHING: SOMETHING: NY | ART DIRECTOR **KEVIN LANDWEHR** | DESIGNER **KEVIN LANDWEHR, DEVIN BECKER, SHOKO TSUJI** ★
CLIENT **CLOAK & DAGGER** | PAPER/MATERIALS **FRENCH PAPER**

★ **NOTHING: SOMETHING: NY** | ART DIRECTOR **KEVIN LANDWEHR** | DESIGNER **KEVIN LANDWEHR, DEVIN BECKER, KEVIN DEVINE**
CLIENT **EDUN-ROGAN, ALI HEWSON, BONO** | PAPER/MATERIALS **PLIKE, KROMEKOTE, LASER CUTTING AND FOIL STAMPING**

NOTHING: SOMETHING: NY | ART DIRECTOR **KEVIN LANDWEHR** | DESIGNER **KEVIN LANDWEHR, DEVIN BECKER**
CLIENT **MADE HER THINK/MEREDITH KAHN**

★

★ **NOTHING: SOMETHING: NY** | ART DIRECTOR **KEVIN LANDWEHR** | DESIGNER **KEVIN LANDWEHR, DEVIN BECKER**
CLIENT **MADE HER THINK/MEREDITH KAHN**

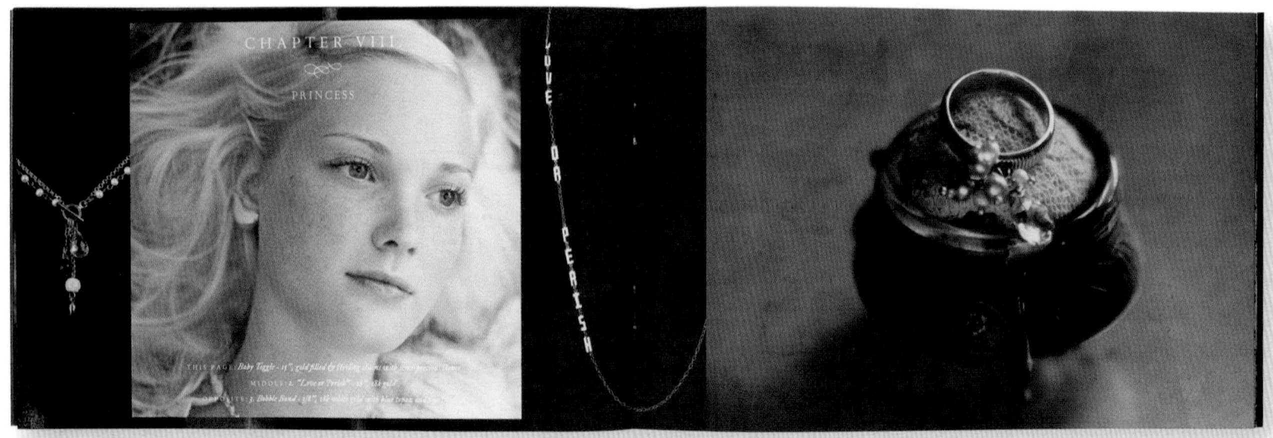

KORN DESIGN | ART DIRECTOR **DENISE KORN** | DESIGNER **MELISSA WEHRMAN** ★
CLIENT **LXR LUXURY RESORTS/THE LONDON NYC HOTEL** | PAPER/MATERIALS **MOHAWK SUPERFINE, MOHAWK NAVAJO**

★ **KORN DESIGN** | ART DIRECTOR **DENISE KORN** | DESIGNER **MELISSA WEHRMAN**
CLIENT **LXR LUXURY RESORTS/THE LONDON NYC HOTEL** | PAPER/MATERIALS **MOHAWK SUPERFINE, MOHAWK NAVAJO**

USA

PROPELLER | ART DIRECTOR **TODD FRIEDMAN, BRIAN EICKHOFF** | DESIGNER **BRIAN EICKHOFF** ★
CLIENT **MAX STRANG ARCHITECTURE** | PAPER/MATERIALS **SHELL: STRATHMORE PREMIUM OPAQUE WHITE SMOOTH 160 LB. COVER, INSERTS: STRATHMORE PREMIUM OPAQUE WHITE SMOOTH 130 LB. COVER**

★ **DESIGN RANCH** | ART DIRECTOR **MICHELLE SONDEREGGER, INGRED SIDIE** | DESIGNER **TAD CARPENTER, RACHEL KARACA**
CLIENT **LEE** | PAPER/MATERIALS **VELLUM AND NEWSPRINT, FRENCH FOLDED AND INDUSTRIAL STAPLED**

USA

LISKA + ASSOCIATES | ART DIRECTOR **STEVE LISKA** | DESIGNER **VANESSA REU, STEVE LISKA** ★
CLIENT **CRANE & CO.** | PAPER/MATERIALS **CRANE'S CREST, 32 LB.**

★ **DESIGNBOLAGET** | ART DIRECTOR **CLAUS DUE** | DESIGNER **CLAUS DUE** | CLIENT **STELLA NOVA**
PAPER/MATERIALS **SLEEVE IN MIRRORBOARD**

DESIGNBOLAGET | ART DIRECTOR **CLAUS DUE** | DESIGNER **CLAUS DUE** | CLIENT **KREBS HYLLESTED** ★
PAPER/MATERIALS **COATED PAPER**

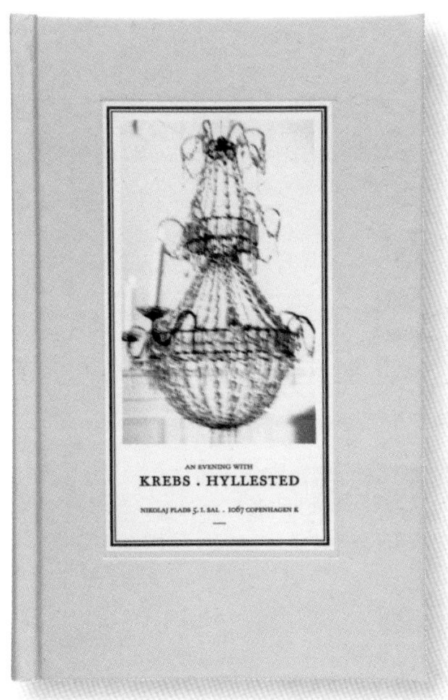

★ **DESIGNBOLAGET** | ART DIRECTOR **CLAUS DUE** | DESIGNER **EMIL GAMMELGAARD, HENRIETTE KRUSE**
CLIENT **WONHUNDRED** | PAPER/MATERIALS **4 DIFFERENT PAPER QUALITIES**

ARE WE THE SAME, WITH
DIFFERENCES?
OR DIFFERENT,
WITH SIMILARITIES?
18–19

- Ten -

★ **ELEVATOR** | ART DIRECTOR **TONY ADAMIC** | DESIGNER **TONY ADAMIC** | CLIENT **NADALINA**
PAPER/MATERIALS **MUNKEN PRINT WHITE 115 GSM, AND 300 GSM**

CROATIA

JKACZMAREK, FALLON | ART DIRECTOR **JESSE KACZMAREK** | DESIGNER **JESSE KACZMAREK** | CLIENT **EARL JEANS** ★

★ **JKACZMAREK, FALLON** | ART DIRECTOR **JESSE KACZMAREK, CRAIG DUFFNEY**
DESIGNER **JESSE KACZMAREK, CRAIG DUFFNEY** | CLIENT **EARL JEANS**

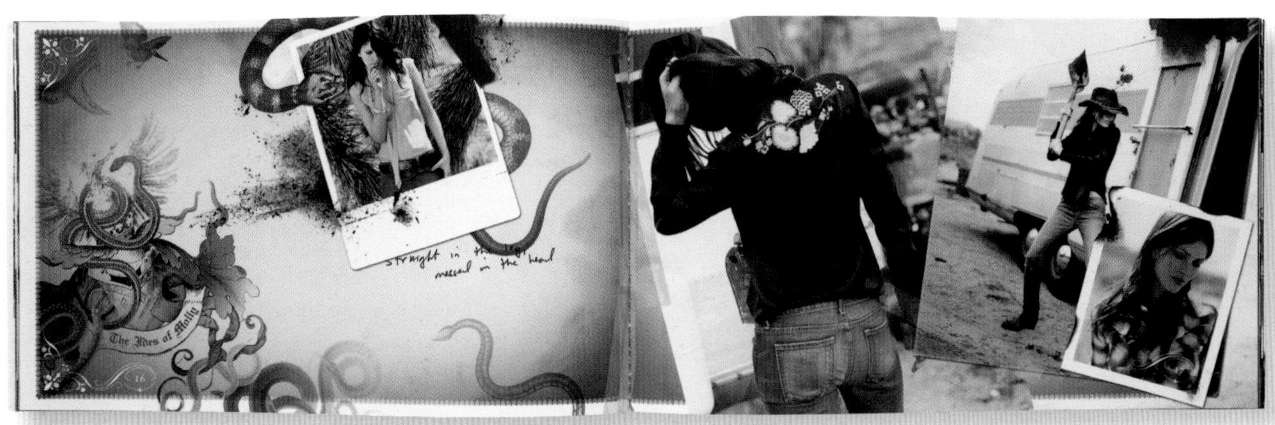

S DESIGN INC. | ART DIRECTOR **SARAH SEARS** | DESIGNER **CARA SANDERS ROBB** | CLIENT **CABA** ★
PAPER/MATERIALS **MOHAWK SUPERFINE**

★ **SK+G ADVERTISING** | ART DIRECTOR **ERIC STEIN, STEVE AVERITT, MIKE MIGLIOZZI** | DESIGNER **HARRY FOREHAND, CHRISTINE TOSTI, ALEX SMITH, KURT SNIDER, BELLE LARSON, CARRI HALL, RAYNA LEE** | CLIENT **PLANET HOLLYWOOD RESORT, LAS VEGAS** | PAPER/MATERIALS **STERLING 100 LB. COVER, FOUR-COLOR PROCESS, EIGHT SPOT COLORS, SPOT VARNISHES**

VANITY (n.) van-i-
ense of extreme pride in one's appearance or abilities, often supported
essive adoration by the masses, ie: "Some people are better looking than everyone else. That's a fact. Why should they pretend like they're not? That's not vanity. It's just the plain truth."

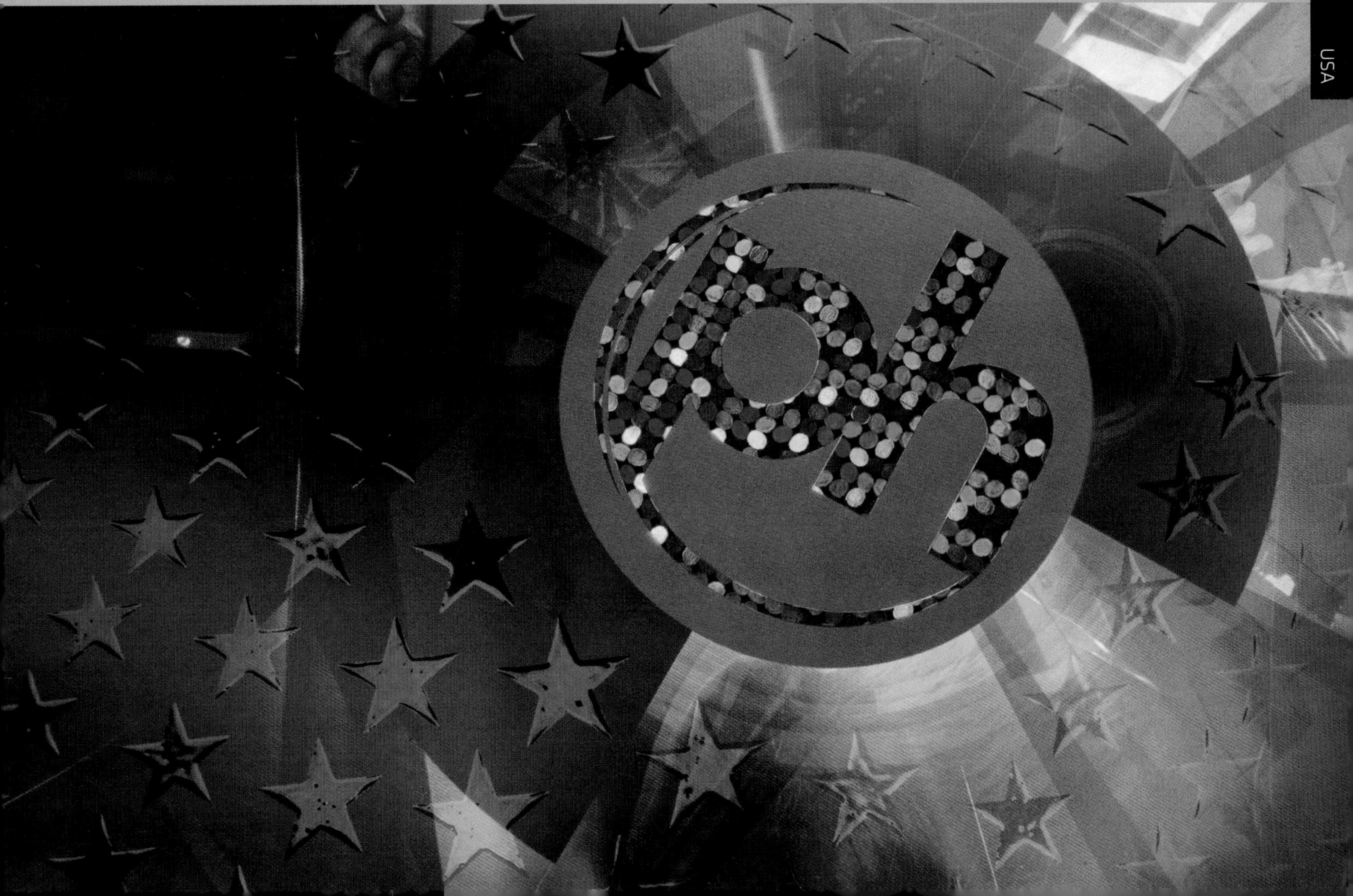

★ **SK+G ADVERTISING** | ART DIRECTOR **STEVE AVERITT, PHILIPP BATALLIA** | DESIGNER **TRACY BROCKHOUSE, BORIS KOSTOV**
CLIENT **FOUR SEASONS OCEAN RESIDENCES** | PAPER/MATERIALS **MOHAWK NAVAHO 65 LB. COVER, SUEDE TEX, YUPO**

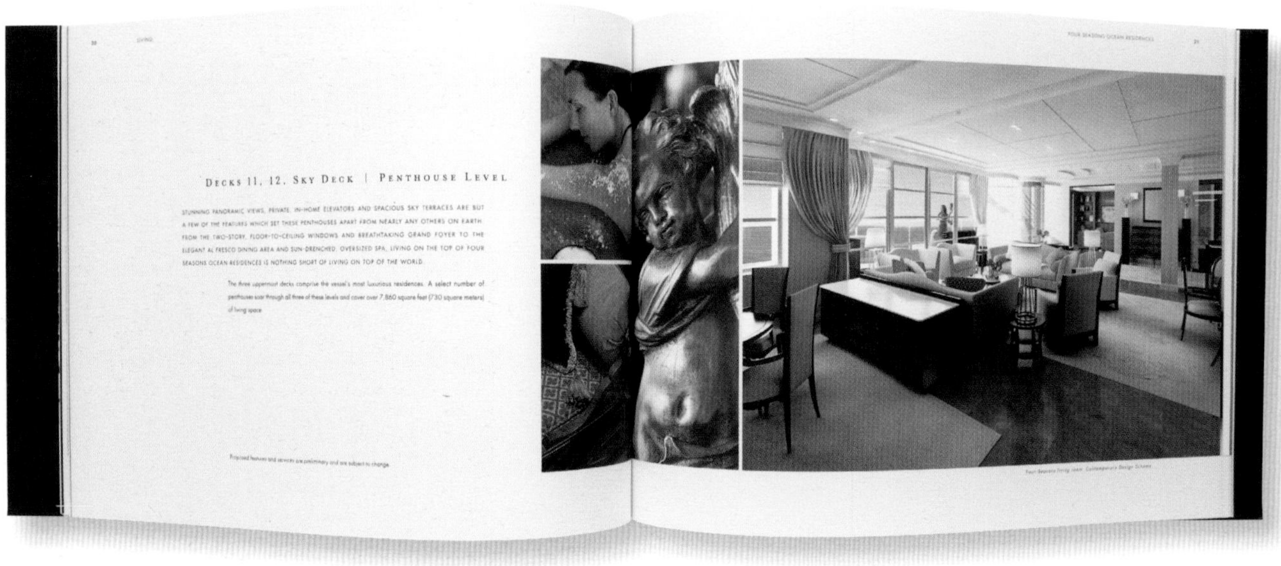

SK+G ADVERTISING | ART DIRECTOR **JEREMY BRISTOL, CLAYTON JAMES, ERIC STEIN** ★
DESIGNER **KURT SNIDER, DIANDRE JOHNSON, MARSHALL AUNE, VANESSA ADAO** | CLIENT **ECHELON, LAS VEGAS**
PAPER/MATERIALS **UTOPIA PREMIUM GLOSS, 100 LB. COVER, FOUR-COLOR PROCESS, FOUR SPOT COLORS, AND SPOT VARNISH**

★ **ENV DESIGN** | ART DIRECTOR **JONAS GROSSMANN** | DESIGNER **JONAS GROSSMANN** | CLIENT **ZEPHYR**

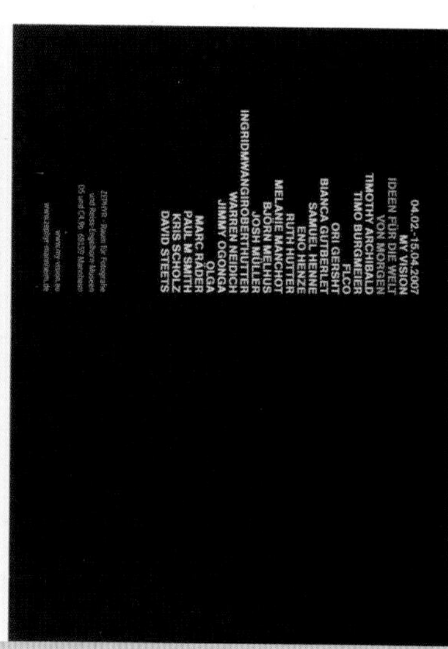

FOLK CREATIVE MARKETING | ART DIRECTOR **ANDREW JENKINSON** | DESIGNER **SIMON HILL** | CLIENT **HIGHLAND**
PAPER/MATERIALS **SILK** ★

UNITED KINGDOM

★ **BANDUJO ADVERTISING AND DESIGN** | ART DIRECTOR **RYOSUKE MATSUMOTO** | CLIENT **GREENBERG TRAURIG, LLP**
PAPER/MATERIALS **MOHAWK NAVAJO BRILLIANT WHITE 65 LB. TEXT, 130 LB. DOUBLE THICK, EXTRA SMOOTH COVER**

USA

BANDUJO ADVERTISING AND DESIGN | ART DIRECTOR **ROBERT BROTHERS** | CLIENT **CITI SMITH BARNEY** ★
PAPER/MATERIALS **MOHAWK NAVAJO BRILLIANT WHITE 120 LB. DOUBLE WEIGHT COVER, 100 LB. TEXT**

★ **CHASE DESIGN GROUP, INC.** | ART DIRECTOR **MARGO CHASE** | DESIGNER **AMY TSUI, TATIANA REDIN, BRIAN HUNT**
CLIENT **CARTOON NETWORK** | PAPER/MATERIALS **TOPKOTE COVER**

CHASE DESIGN GROUP, INC. | ART DIRECTOR **MARGO CHASE** | DESIGNER **STEPHANIE RUBIN, MARIA GAVIRRIA, CLARK GOOLSBY, AMÉLIE BONET** | CLIENT **CARTOON NETWORK** | PAPER/MATERIALS **MCCOY SILK TEXT** ★

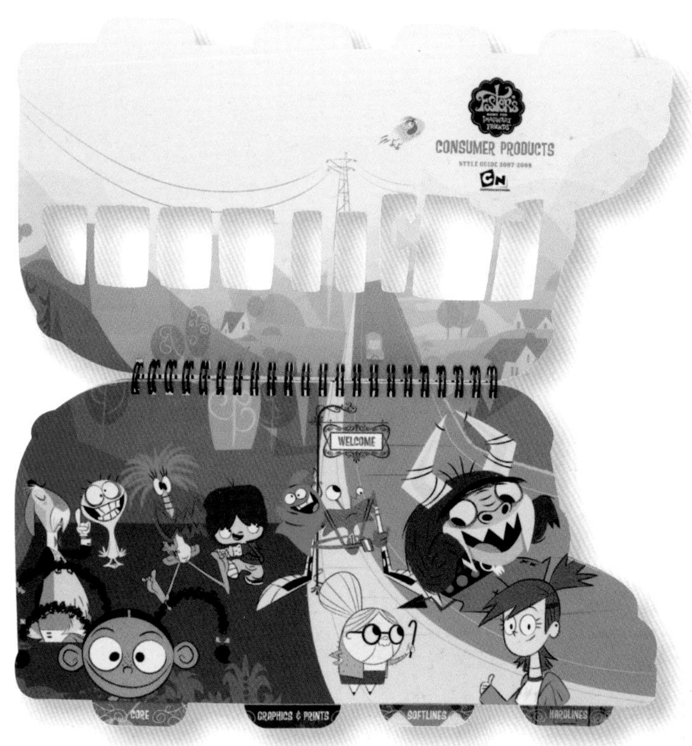

USA

★ **MILTON GLASER, INC.** | ART DIRECTOR **MILTON GLASER** | DESIGNER **DEBORAH ADLER** | CLIENT **SUNY STONYBROOK**
PAPER/MATERIALS **80 LB. MOHAWK TRUE WHITE SMOOTH COVER, 70 LB. MOHAWK TRUE WHITE VELLUM TEXT**

USA

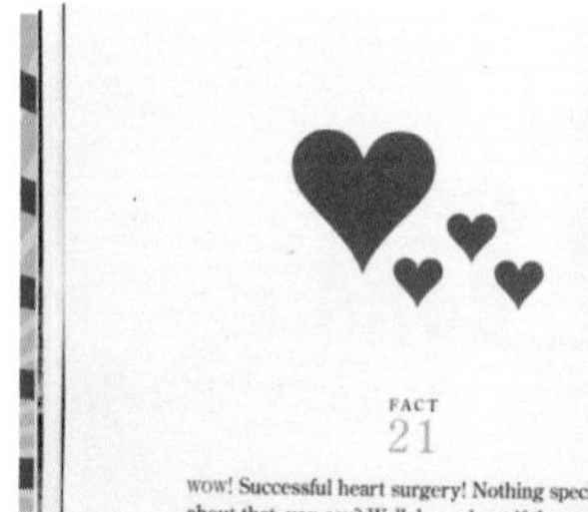

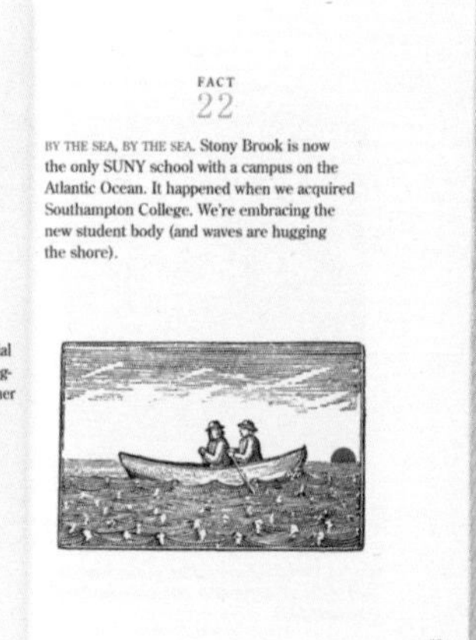

WICKED CREATIVE | ART DIRECTOR **GABRIEL GARCIA** | DESIGNER **GABRIEL GARCIA** | CLIENT **L5**
PAPER/MATERIALS **TOPKOTE GLOSS** ★

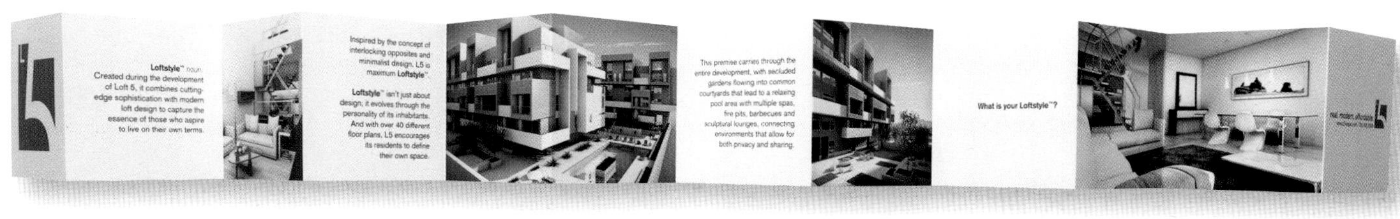

★ **SAATCHI DESIGN** | ART DIRECTOR **KEVIN FINN, JULIAN MELHUISH** | CLIENT **SPICERS PAPER**

SAATCHI DESIGN | ART DIRECTOR **KEVIN FINN, JULIAN MELHUISH** | CLIENT **SPICERS PAPER** | ★

Actually, you're holding it.

Splendorgel. Strange name. Serious paper.

★ **EBD** | ART DIRECTOR **ELLEN BRUSS** | DESIGNER **JORGE LAMORA, CHARLES CARPENTER**
CLIENT **ZI LOFTS AND TOWNHOMES** | PAPER/MATERIALS **NEENAH CLASSIC CREST AND TINTED SPOT VARNISH**

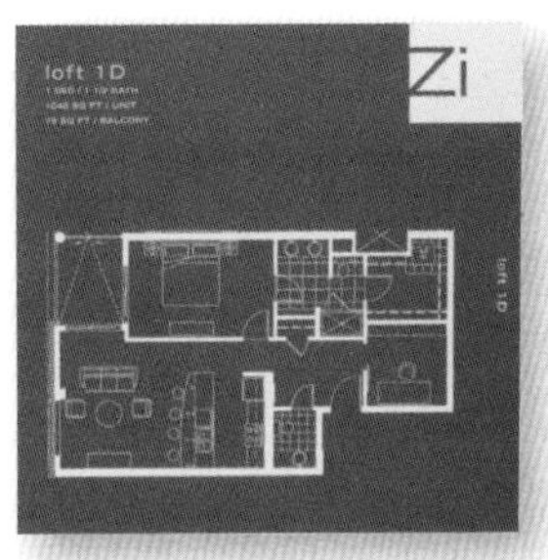

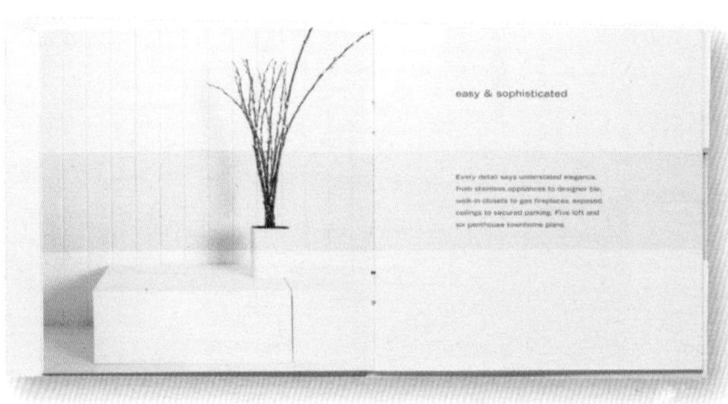

NEO DESIGN | ART DIRECTOR **CRAIG HUTTON** | DESIGNER **CRAIG HUTTON, PAUL HOLLINGWORTH** ★
CLIENT **CONCEPT PERSONNEL** | PAPER/MATERIALS **COVER: SUPER BUFF, 350 GSM, TEXT: CHALLENGER OFFSET, 150 GSM**

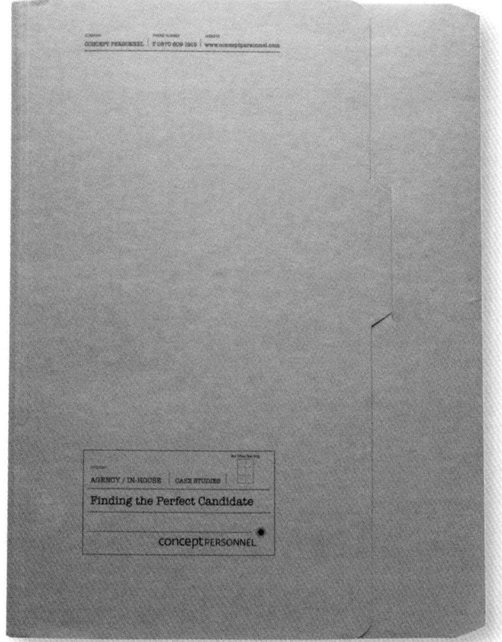

★ **JOHNSTON DUFFY** | ART DIRECTOR **MARTIN DUFFY** | DESIGNER **MARTIN DUFFY** | CLIENT **THE W GROUP**
PAPER/MATERIALS **SCHEUFELEN PHOENIXMOTION**

JOHNSTON DUFFY | ART DIRECTOR **MARTIN DUFFY** | DESIGNER **MARTIN DUFFY** | CLIENT **WONDERBOY CLOTHING** ★
PAPER/MATERIALS **DIAMOND SILK TEXT, MOHAWK SUPERFINE**

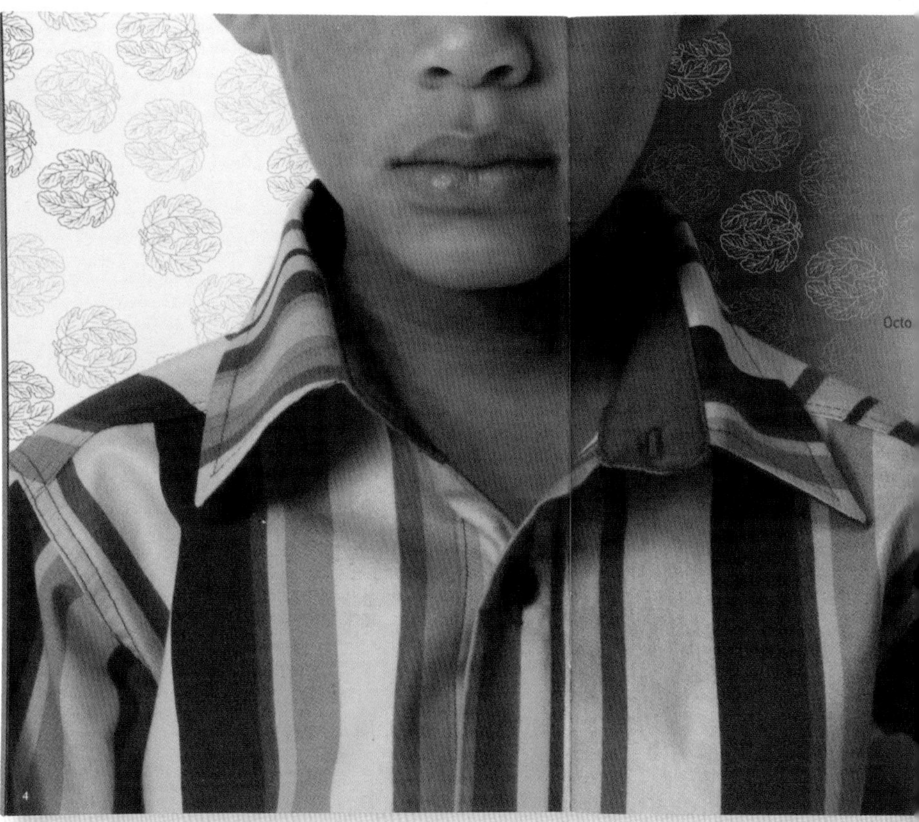

★ **JOHNSTON DUFFY** | ART DIRECTOR **MARTIN DUFFY** | DESIGNER **MARTIN DUFFY** | CLIENT **WONDERBOY CLOTHING**
PAPER/MATERIALS **DIAMOND SILK, DULL AQUEOUS COATING**

JOHNSTON DUFFY | ART DIRECTOR **MARTIN DUFFY** | DESIGNER **ANDY EVANS, MARTIN DUFFY** ★
CLIENT **WONDERBOY CLOTHING** | PAPER/MATERIALS **SCHEUFELEN CONSORT ROYAL BRILLIANCE BLUE WHITE**

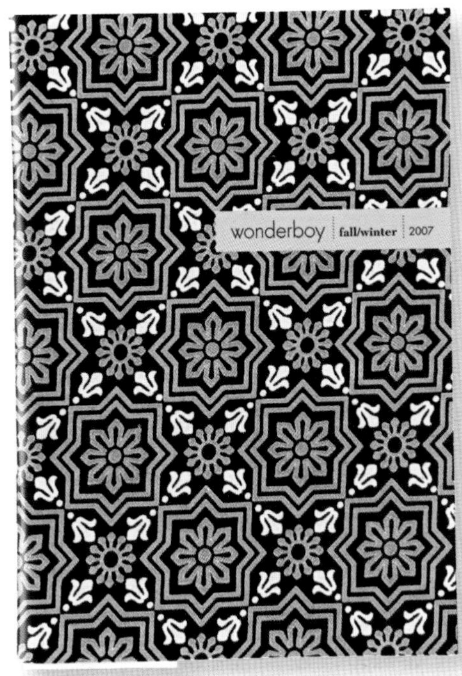

★ **KOLEGRAM** | ART DIRECTOR **GONTRAN BLAIS** | DESIGNER **GONTRAN BLAIS** | CLIENT **BUNTIN REID**

YOU'RE INVITED

WE TOLD 10 PEOPLE
THAT *Buntin Reid*
IS HAVING ANOTHER
PAPER SHOW AT
THE HARD ROCK CAFÉ
AND THIS IS WHAT
THEY HAD TO SAY:

ROYCROFT DESIGN | ART DIRECTOR **JENNIFER ROYCROFT** | DESIGNER **JENNIFER ROYCROFT** | CLIENT **AQUENT** ★

I've got twice the work, half the staff, and no budget to grow my team. | We launch one new product, and the next one's already rolling through the door. | We've got the marketing strategy. Now who can help us execute? | With so many audience segments, I need multiple executions of the same creative. Fast. | Our Web site looks great, but it's not generating enough revenue. | My customer base is constantly shifting. How do I learn what makes them tick?

We hear you

AQUENT

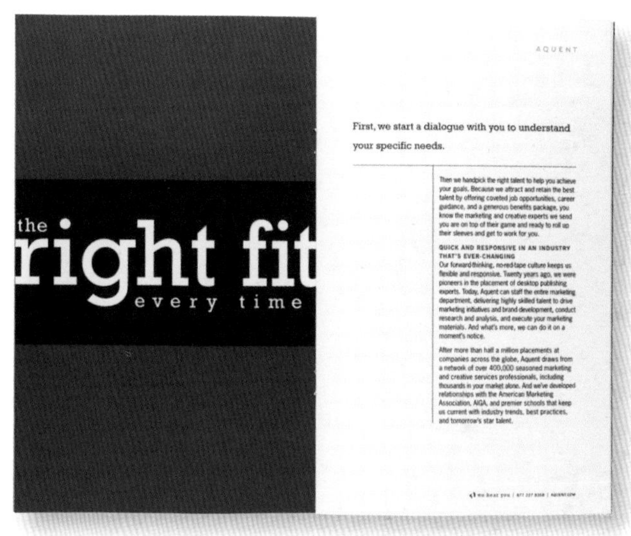

★ **CONNIE HWANG DESIGN** | ART DIRECTOR **CONNIE HWANG** | DESIGNER **CONNIE HWANG**
CLIENT **UNIVERSITY GALLERIES** | PAPER/MATERIALS **STERLING ULTRA GLOSS COVER, GILCLEAR**

SHINE ADVERTISING | ART DIRECTOR **MICHAEL KRIEFSKI** | DESIGNER **BRADLEY GUTTING** ★

CLIENT **AUBURN RIDGE** | PAPER/MATERIALS **COVER: GILBERT OXFORD SMOKED, TEXT: PHOENIX MOTION, XANTUR**

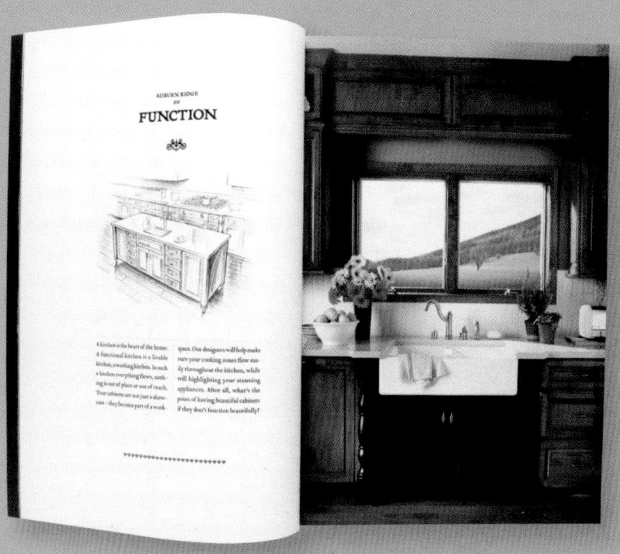

OUR STORY

An idea. A vision. A dream.

In 1898 the brand that would become Auburn Ridge began, like most things begin, with an idea, a vision, a dream. From an old lumbermill to an innovative cabinet workshop, decades of tradition and craftsmanship seep through every inch of our building. The smell of freshly cut timber continues to permeate the air. Layers of sawdust fill the nooks and crannies, and like the rings of a tree, tell our history. These beautifully handcrafted kitchens, cabinets, and millwork designs are the product of this history.

These cabinets you see before you; they are cabinets built by craftsmen who still work with their hands – who cut and finish and create with their hands because they know their hands. They know machines can't feel the grain in a piece of wood. They know machines don't feel pride in what they've made.

These cabinets are the result of people believing what they do is more than manufacturing, that it is indeed, an art. They are the result of a company committed to doing things the right way. Because when all is said and done, it's the only way that really works. It always has been, and it always will be.

★ **THE CHASE** | ART DIRECTOR **STEPHEN ROYLE** | DESIGNER **STEPHEN ROYLE, LIZZIE CAMERON**
CLIENT **LAND SECURITIES**

DESIGN CENTER LTD. | ART DIRECTOR **EDUARD CEHOVIN** | DESIGNER **EDUARD CEHOVIN** | CLIENT **KRATER GROUP** ★

★ IN THIS SECTION

ARTS

★ **TOMATO KOŠIR S.P.** | ART DIRECTOR **TOMATO KOŠIR** | DESIGNER **TOMATO KOŠIR** | CLIENT **SLOVENIAN FILM FUND**
PAPER/MATERIALS **GARDA MATT WHITE, 120 & 300 GSM**

DESIGN ARMY | ART DIRECTOR **PUM LEFEBURE, JAKE LEFEBURE** | DESIGNER **MIKE MALUSO** ★
CLIENT **BLACK BOOK PUBLISHING** | PAPER/MATERIALS **HARD BOUND BOOK**

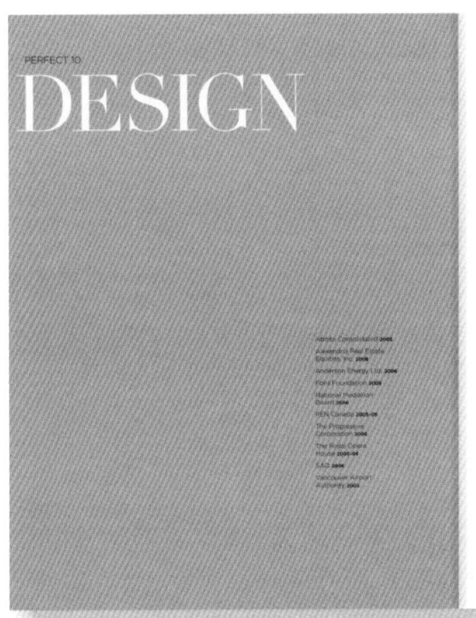

★ **WECHSLER** | ART DIRECTOR **MIKE HALL** | DESIGNER **MIKE HALL, AARON SHAW** | CLIENT **MUSEUM OF ARMY FLYING**

VISITOR INF

CORPORATE DAYS

THE MUSE
Middle Wallop

EVENTS

THE MUSEUM OF ARMY FLYING
Middle Wallop Stockbridge Hampshire SO20 8DY

★ **RYSZARD BIENERT** | ART DIRECTOR **RYSZARD BIENERT** | DESIGNER **RYSZARD BIENERT** | CLIENT **GALERIA PIEKARY 5**
PAPER/MATERIALS **COVER: 3 MM CARDBOARD, SILKSCREEN PRINTED WITH METALLIC PANTONE, UV SPOT VARNISH, STEEL STAPLED, FINISHED WITH CANVAS SPINE**

RYSZARD BIENERT | ART DIRECTOR **RYSZARD BIENERT** | DESIGNER **RYSZARD BIENERT** | CLIENT **MUZEUM ZIEMI LUBUSKIEJ** ★
PAPER/MATERIALS **COVER: DEBOSSING ON HANDMADE PAPER, INSIDE: COATED, UNCOATED STOCK, METALLIC PAPER**

★ **RYSZARD BIENERT** | ART DIRECTOR **RYSZARD BIENERT** | DESIGNER **RYSZARD BIENERT** | CLIENT **GALERIA PIEKARY 5**

SUBSTANCE151 | ART DIRECTOR **IDA CHEINMAN** | DESIGNER **IDA CHEINMAN, RICK SALZMAN** ★
CLIENT **ADVERTISING ASSOCIATION OF BALTIMORE** | PAPER/MATERIALS **FINCH FINE COVER AND TEXT, EMBOSSING**

★ **HANGAR 18 CREATIVE GROUP** | ART DIRECTOR **SEAN CARTER** | DESIGNER **TODD CHAPMAN** | CLIENT **UNISOURCE**

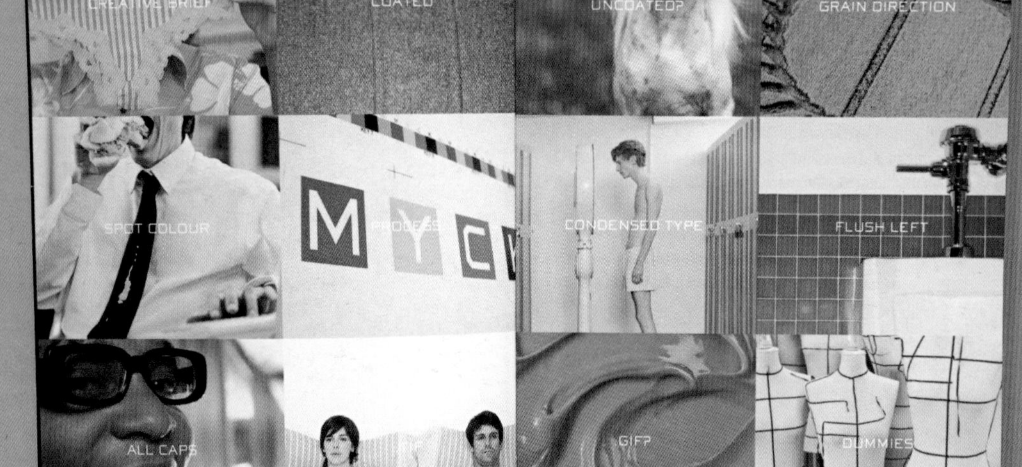

HANGAR 18 CREATIVE GROUP | ART DIRECTOR **SEAN CARTER** | DESIGNER **TODD CHAPMAN** | CLIENT **UNISOURCE** ★

INSPIRED. ORIGINAL. DETAILED. THOUGHTFUL. CRAFTED. SMART. INFLUENTIAL. DESIGN THAT PROVOKES, CHALLENGES, ALTERS OUR EXPECTATIONS OF WHAT AN ANNUAL REPORT OR BROCHURE *SHOULD* BE. UNISOURCE IS ONCE AGAIN CELEBRATING EXCEPTIONAL DESIGN WORK WITH NUARS 2007.

INSPIRÉ. ORIGINAL. MINUTIEUX. RÉFLÉCHI. OUVRAGÉ. SOIGNÉ. INFLUENT. DESIGN QUI PROVOQUE, DÉFIE, CHANGE NOTRE PERCEPTION DE CE QUE *DEVRAIT* ÊTRE UN RAPPORT ANNUEL OU UNE BROCHURE. UNISOURCE SOULIGNE DE NOUVEAU LES PROJETS DE CONCEPTION EXCEPTIONNELS AVEC NUARS 2007.

THE RULES/LES RÈGLEMENTS

GREAT DESIGN

CHALLENGES EXPECTED THINKING.

THE 2007 NATIONAL UNISOURCE ANNUAL REPORT SHOW

NU·aR^S

CANADA

★ **SAGMEISTER, INC.** | ART DIRECTOR **STEFAN SAGMEISTER** | DESIGNER **JOE SHOULDICE**
CLIENT **KUNSTHAUS BREGENT** | PAPER/MATERIALS **NEWSPRINT**

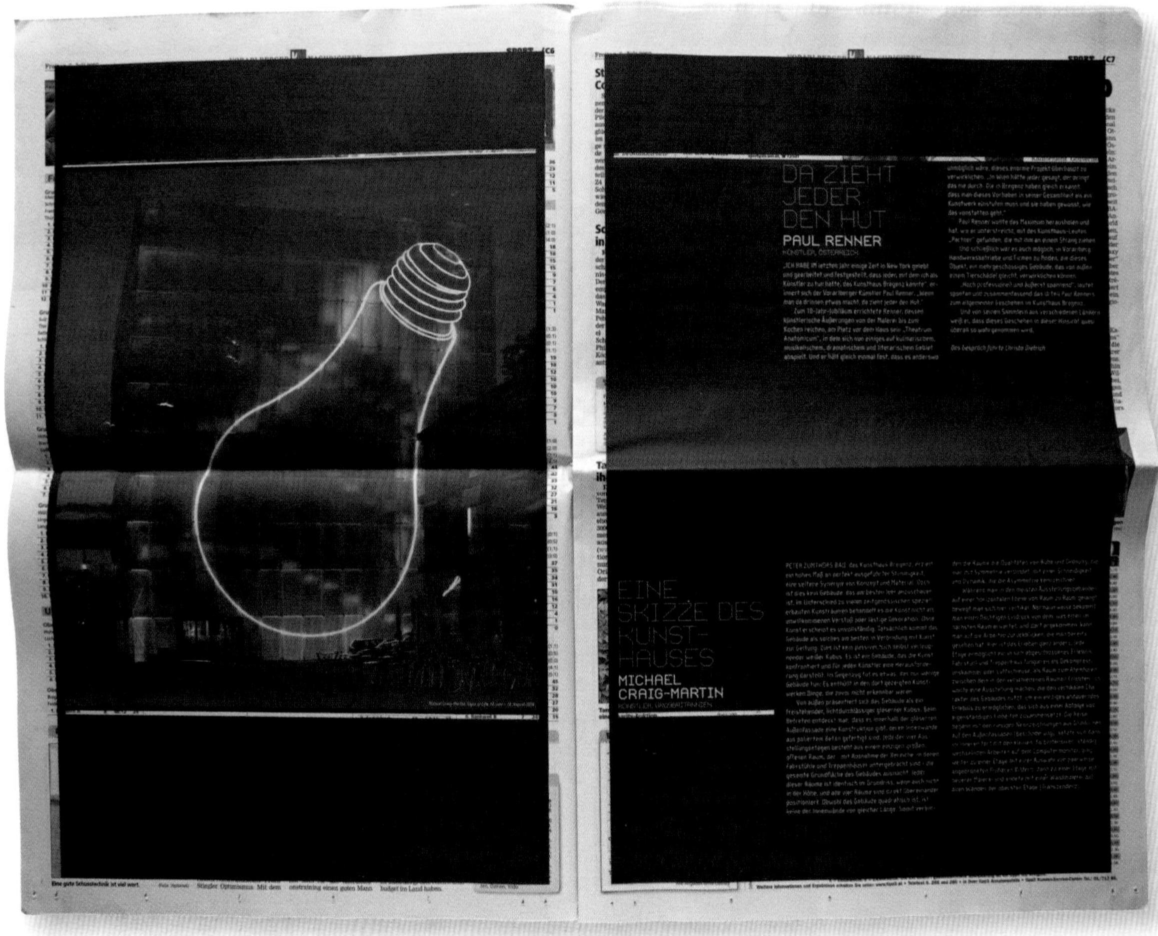

DESIGN ONE | ART DIRECTOR **JIM SLATTON** | DESIGNER **JIM SLATTON** | CLIENT **THE FURNITURE SOCIETY** ★
PAPER/MATERIALS **COVER: ROYAL FIBER, 80 LB., TEXT: UTOPIA 2 MATTE 100 LB., 6" × 9" (15.2 × 22.9 cm) MYLAR BAG**

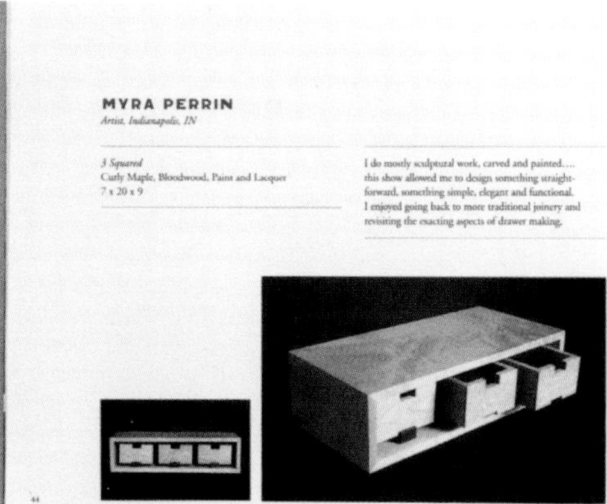

MYRA PERRIN
Artist, Indianapolis, IN

3 Squared
Curly Maple, Bloodwood, Paint and Lacquer
7 x 20 x 9

I do mostly sculptural work, carved and painted.... this show allowed me to design something straight-forward, something simple, elegant and functional. I enjoyed going back to more traditional joinery and revisiting the exacting aspects of drawer making.

WILLIAM PICKFORD
Studio Furniture Maker, Rindge, NH

Offering
Mahogany, White Oak, Reclaimed Flooring and Ebony
40 x 28 x 18

This piece originated with a project at Rochester Institute of Technology that had to do with the source of inspiration for a drawer. I chose to focus on horror movies I had watched and I wanted to capture an eerie feeling on the exterior with an uplifting ending when you open the drawer. I have titled this piece *Offering* in hope that the viewer is able to take my concept and create their own narrative.

★ **AUFULDISH & WARRINER** | ART DIRECTOR **BOB AUFULDISH** | DESIGNER **BOB AUFULDISH, KATHERINE WARRINER**
CLIENT **SWA GROUP** | PAPER/MATERIALS **VARIOUS**

USA

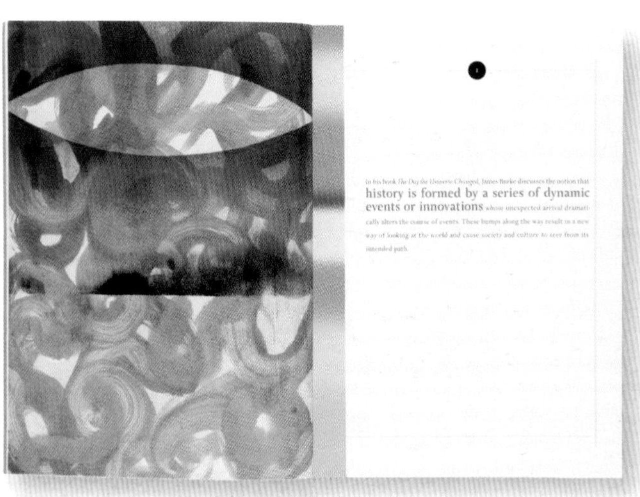

DESIGNBOLAGET | ART DIRECTOR **CLAUS DUE** | DESIGNER **CLAUS DUE** | CLIENT **BAUM UND PFERDGARTEN** ★
PAPER/MATERIALS **UNCOATED PAPER**

★ **AUFULDISH & WARRINER** | ART DIRECTOR **BOB AUFULDISH** | DESIGNER **BOB AUFULDISH, KATHERINE WARRINER**
CLIENT **SWA GROUP** | PAPER/MATERIALS **UNCOATED PAPER**

TOKY BRANDING + DESIGN | ART DIRECTOR **ERIC THOELKE** | DESIGNER **KATY FISCHER** ★
CLIENT **CONTEMPORARY ART MUSEUM, ST. LOUIS**

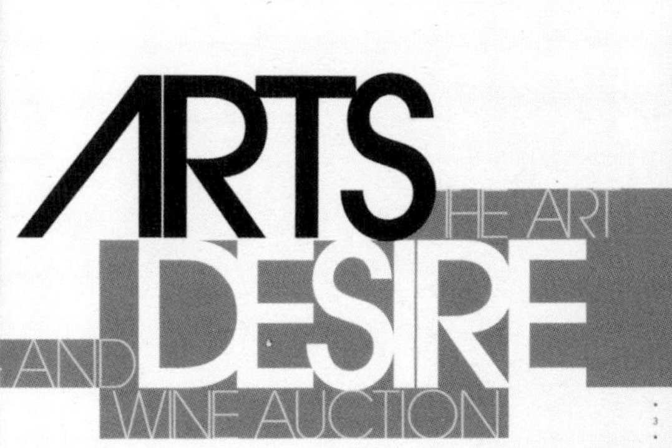

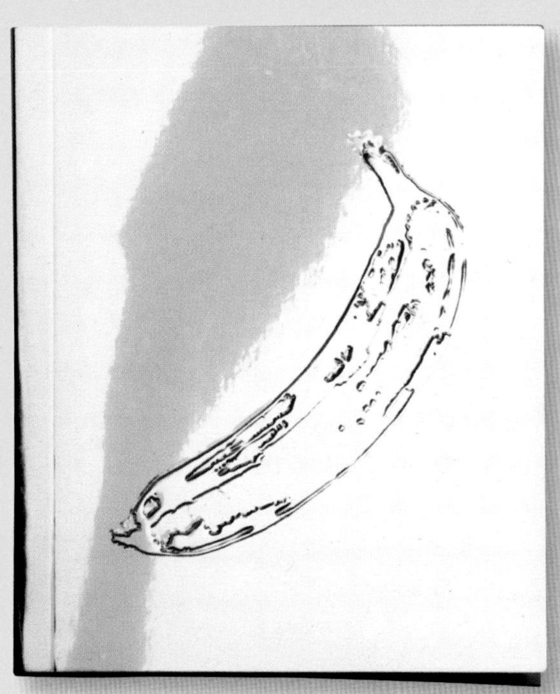

★ **DESIGNBOLAGET** | ART DIRECTOR **CLAUS DUE** | DESIGNER **CLAUS DUE** | CLIENT **SUMO**
PAPER/MATERIALS **SLEEVE: CARDBOARD, TEXT: COATED PAPER**

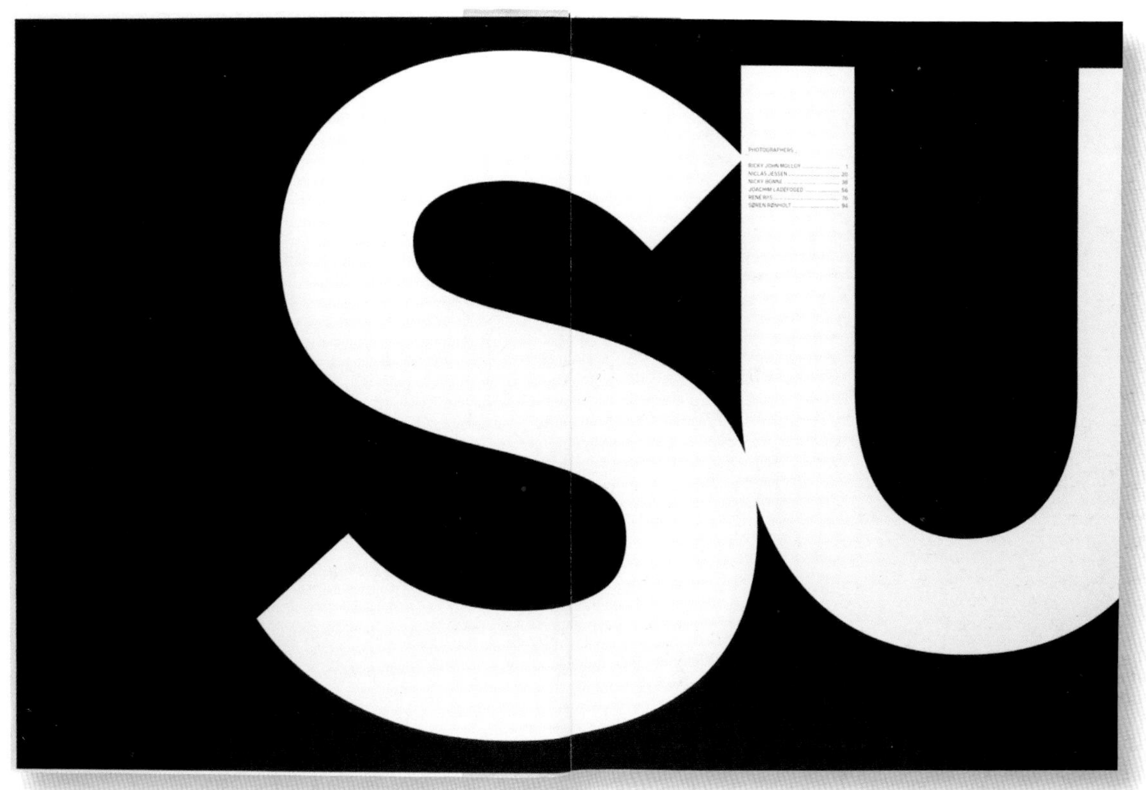
SU
PHOTOGRAPHERS
RICKY JOHN MOLLOY 1
NICLAS JESSEN 20
NICKY BONNE 38
JOACHIM LADEFOGED 56
RENÉ RIIS 76
SØREN RØNHOLT 94

★ **RIGSBY HULL** | ART DIRECTOR **THOMAS HULL, LANA RIGSBY** | DESIGNER **THOMAS HULL** | CLIENT **CAROL PIPER RUGS**
PAPER/MATERIALS **SCHEUFELEN PHOENIXMOTION**

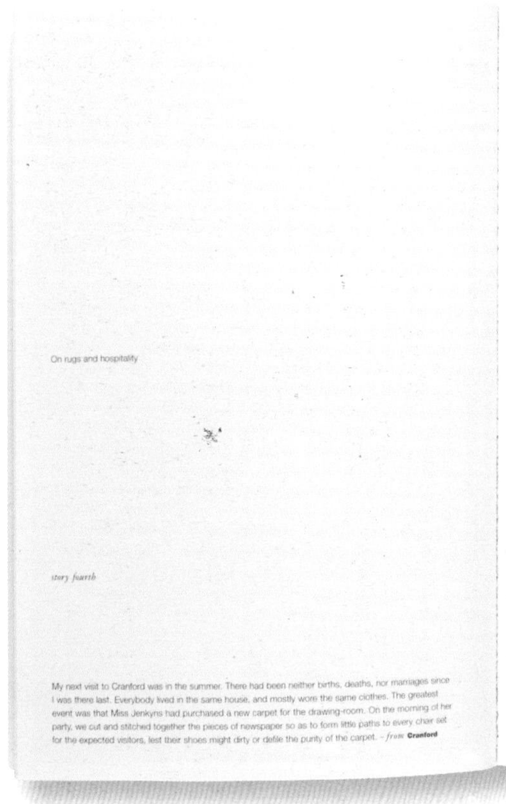

EBD | ART DIRECTOR **ELLEN BRUSS** | DESIGNER **JORGE LAMORA** | CLIENT **MUSEUM OF CONTEMPORARY ART, DENVER** ★
PAPER/MATERIALS **VELLUM SLEEVE**

USA

★ **CONNIE HWANG DESIGN** | ART DIRECTOR **CONNIE HWANG** | DESIGNER **CONNIE HWANG**
CLIENT **UNIVERSITY GALLERIES** | PAPER/MATERIALS **MOHAWK SUPERFINE, EAMES**

USA

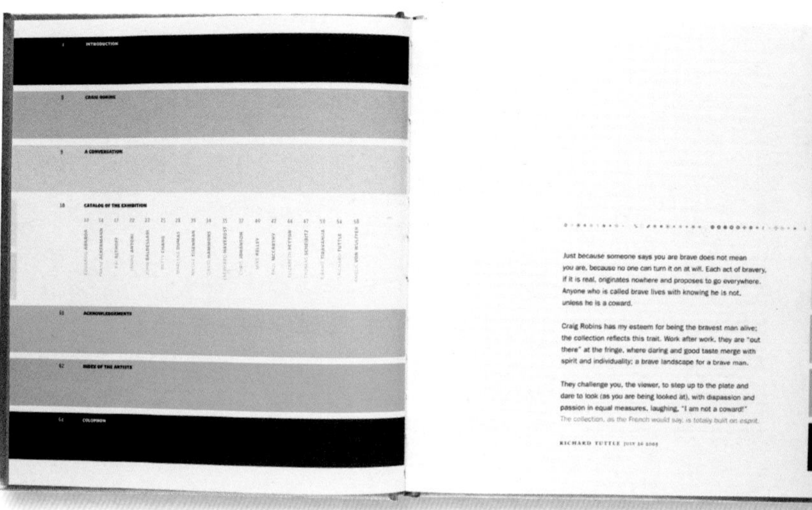

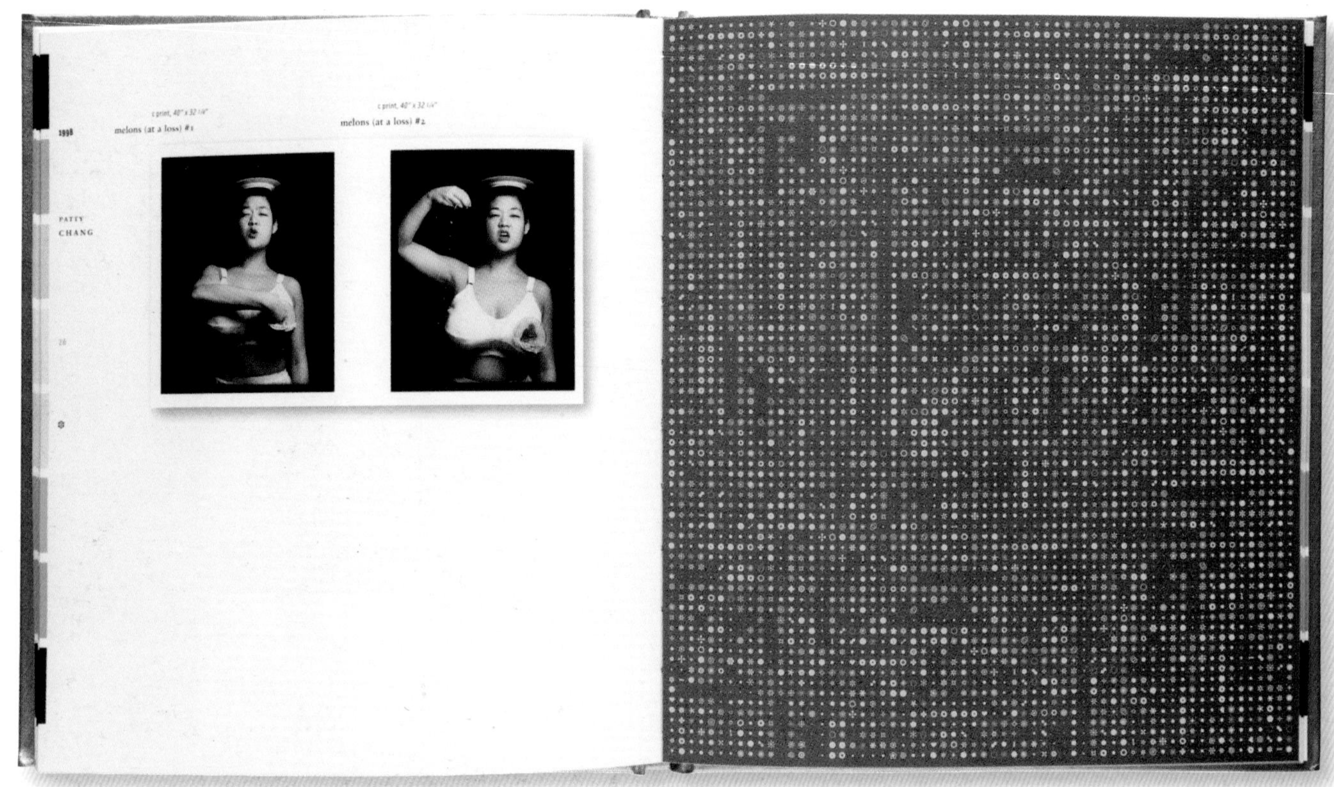

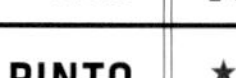

KARACTERS DESIGN GROUP | ART DIRECTOR **ERIC NIELSEN, JOHN FURNEAUX** | DESIGNER **ERIN HEALEY, CHRISTINA PINTO**
CLIENT **RGD ONTARIO** | PAPER/MATERIALS **WEYERHAEUSER COUGAR OPAQUE**

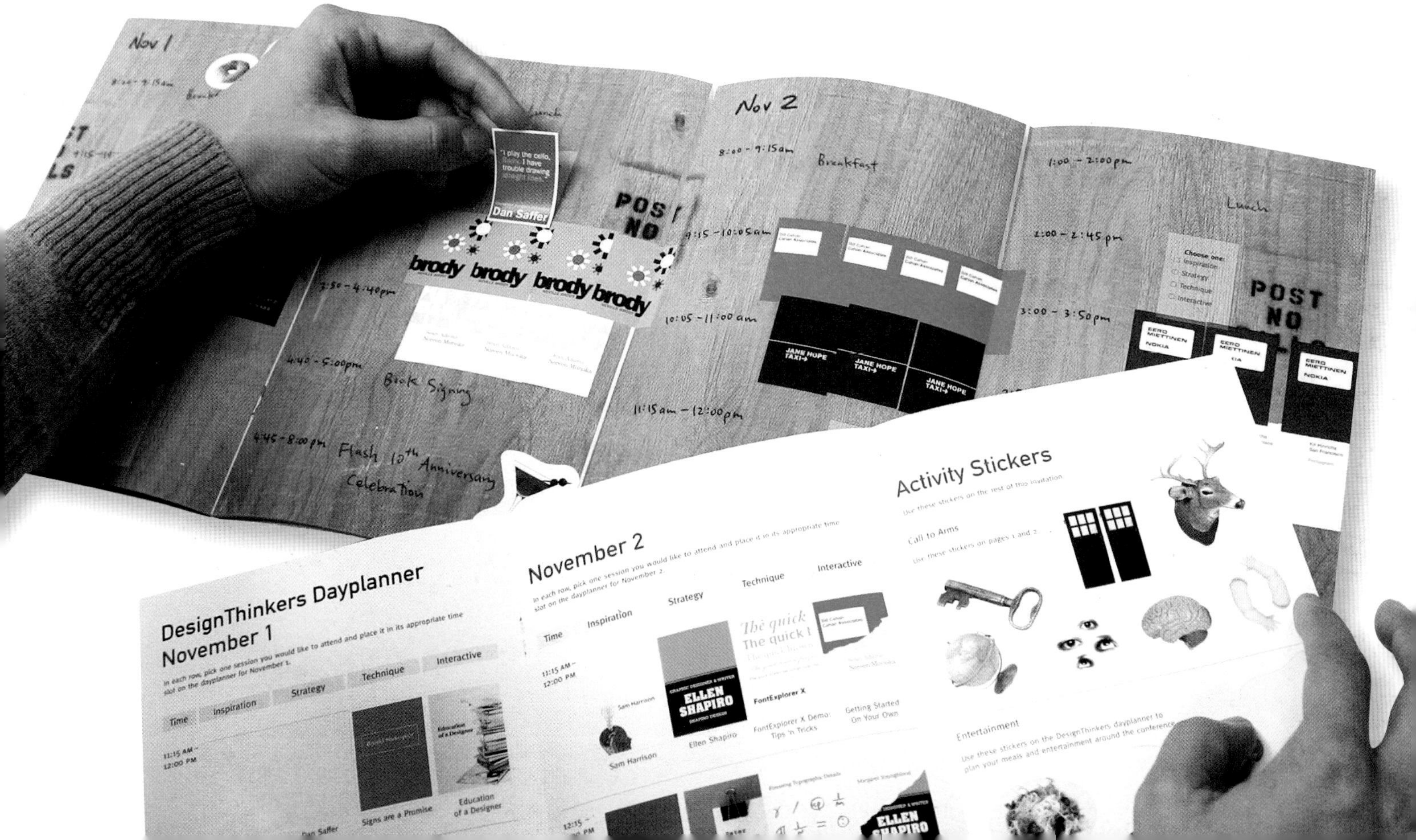

★ **LUKAS HUFFMAN** | ART DIRECTOR **LUKAS HUFFMAN** | DESIGNER **LUKAS HUFFMAN** | CLIENT **PULP PUBLISHING**
PAPER/MATERIALS **COVER: IRIS BROADCLOTH WHITE, TEXT: 100 LB. ACCENT OPAQUE WHITE, 100 LB. TOPKOTE GLOSS AND DULL BOOK WHITE, 80 LB., 100 LB. ACCENT VELLUM BOOK WHITE, ENDSHEETS: 100 LB. ACCENT OPAQUE WHITE**

...a reminder that
we
are
weak,

USA

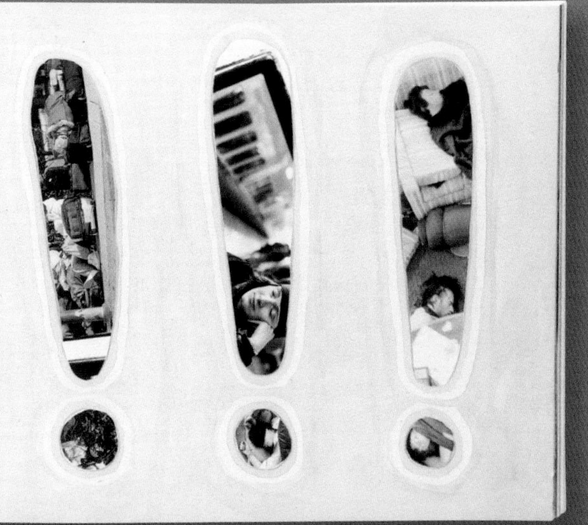

It'scrowds
flashesfa
graphsat
complim
ousex
richfort
eternalin
danger
tiveconfu
revealing
insecure
tisticaldel
lonely. It's

★ **DESIGN ARMY** | ART DIRECTOR **PUM LEFEBURE, JAKE LEFEBURE** | DESIGNER **DAN ADLER**
CLIENT **SIGNATURE THEATRE** | PAPER/MATERIALS **FINCH FINE**

USA

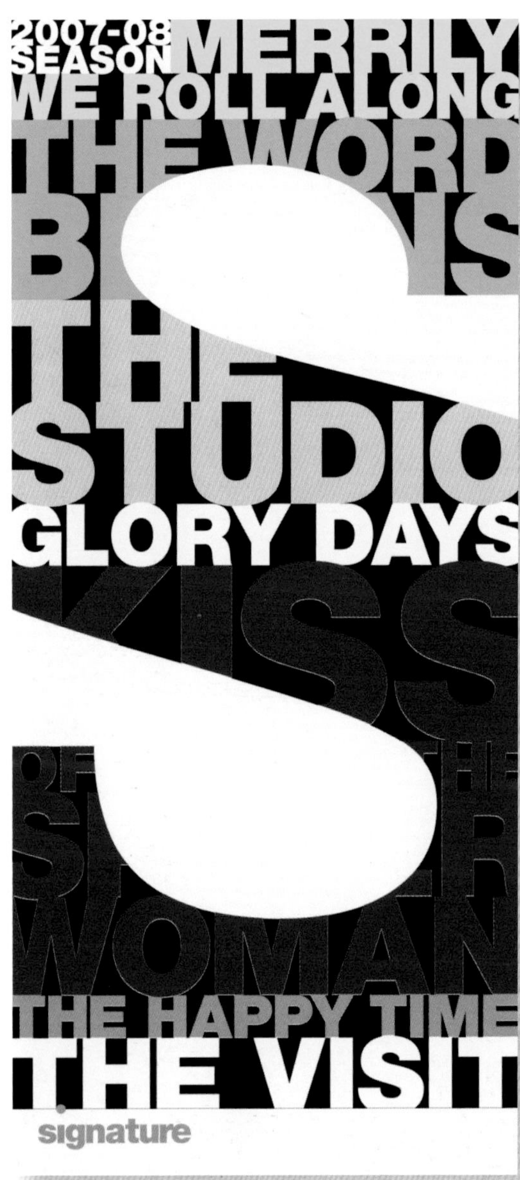

DESIGN ARMY | ART DIRECTOR **PUM LEFEBURE, JAKE LEFEBURE** | DESIGNER **DAN ADLER** ★
CLIENT **SIGNATURE THEATRE** | PAPER/MATERIALS **FINCH FINE, CARNIVAL LINEN, DIE CUT JACKET, FOIL STAMPING**

act one
history

Live, Laugh, Love
I remember when my friend Dick Gommersall and I first walked through the old garage on Four Mile Run Drive. We had to go through about four inches of water just to get into the building. We finally got in the back door to find it was flooded inside. I looked up and saw the sky — not a roof. Rats were running in the shadows. But I also saw all these industrial girders, and the strength in the building. Right away I knew this could be something. I think the first words out of Dick's mouth were, "Eric, are you nuts?" I replied, "Probably. But don't you think this is going to be a great theater?" I was able to convince him that with a lot of hard work, and his brilliance as an architect, we could turn the old garage into a great theater space. And we did.

– Eric

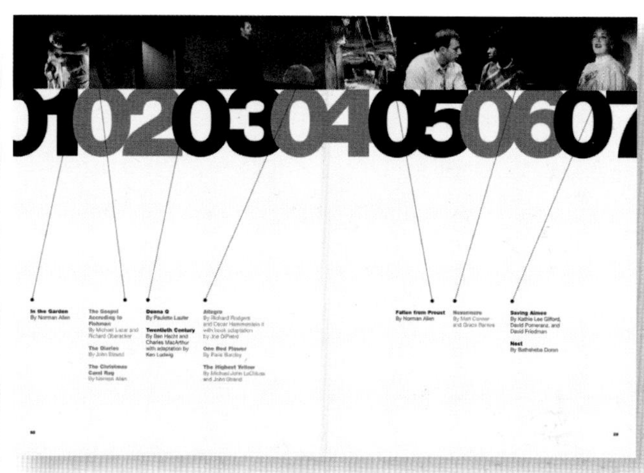

USA

★ IN THIS SECTION

RETHINK

BILLY BLUE CREATIVE

KYM ABRAMS DESIGN

GDC—GUGLIELMINO DESIGN CO.

CREATIVE SPARK

WALLACE CHURCH, INC.

GRAPHICULTURE

MIRKO ILIĆ CORP.

LLOYDS GRAPHIC DESIGN LTD.

PROPELLER

LISKA + ASSOCIATES

DAVID CARTER DESIGN ASSOCIATES

THIELEN DESIGNS, INC.

IE DESIGN + COMMUNICATIONS

SAGMEISTER, INC.

ANNABELLE GOULD DESIGN

NEO DESIGN

SELF-PROMOTIONAL

★ **RETHINK** | CREATIVE DIRECTOR **IAN GRAIS, CHRIS STAPLES** | DESIGNER **ISABELLE SWIDERSKI, STEVE PINTER**
CLIENT **CAPIC** | PAPER/MATERIALS **100 LB. PRODUCTOLITH MATTE COVER, 100 LB. PRODUCTOLITH GLOSS TEXT**

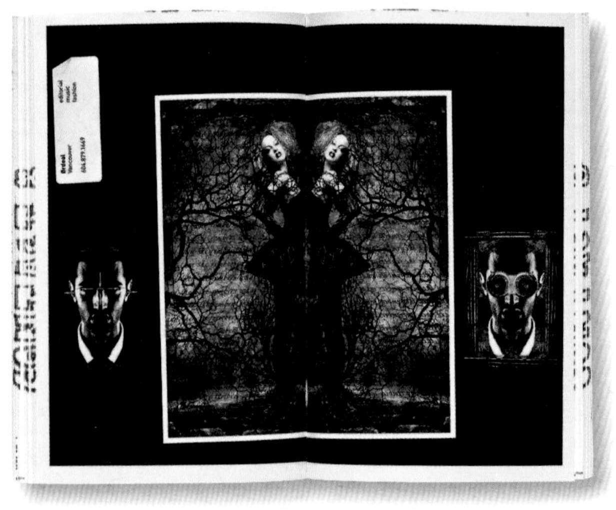

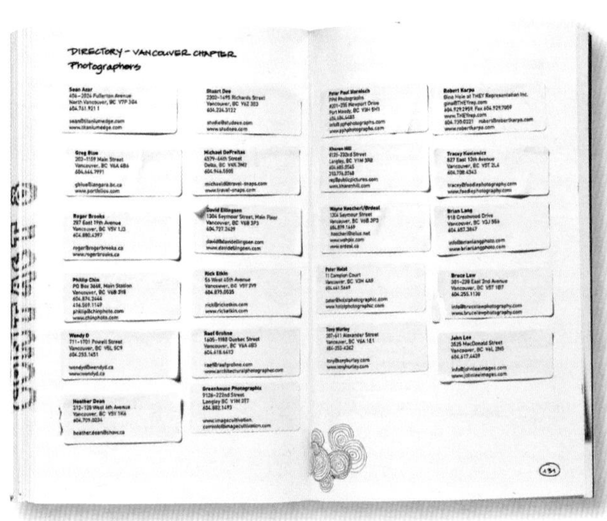

BILLY BLUE CREATIVE | ART DIRECTOR **JUSTIN SMITH** | DESIGNER **JUSTIN SMITH** | CLIENT **BILLY BLUE GROUP** ★

★ **KYM ABRAMS DESIGN** | ART DIRECTOR **KYM ABRAMS** | DESIGNER **MELISSA DEPASQUALE**
CLIENT **ERIKSON INSTITUTE** | PAPER/MATERIALS **MOHAWK SUPERFINE**

GDC–GUGLIELMINO DESIGN CO. | ART DIRECTOR **SID GUGLIELMINO** | DESIGNER **JAMES BELL** ★
CLIENT **GDC–GUGLIELMINO DESIGN CO.** | PAPER/MATERIALS **NOVATECH SATIN AND CROMATICO EXTRA WHITE**

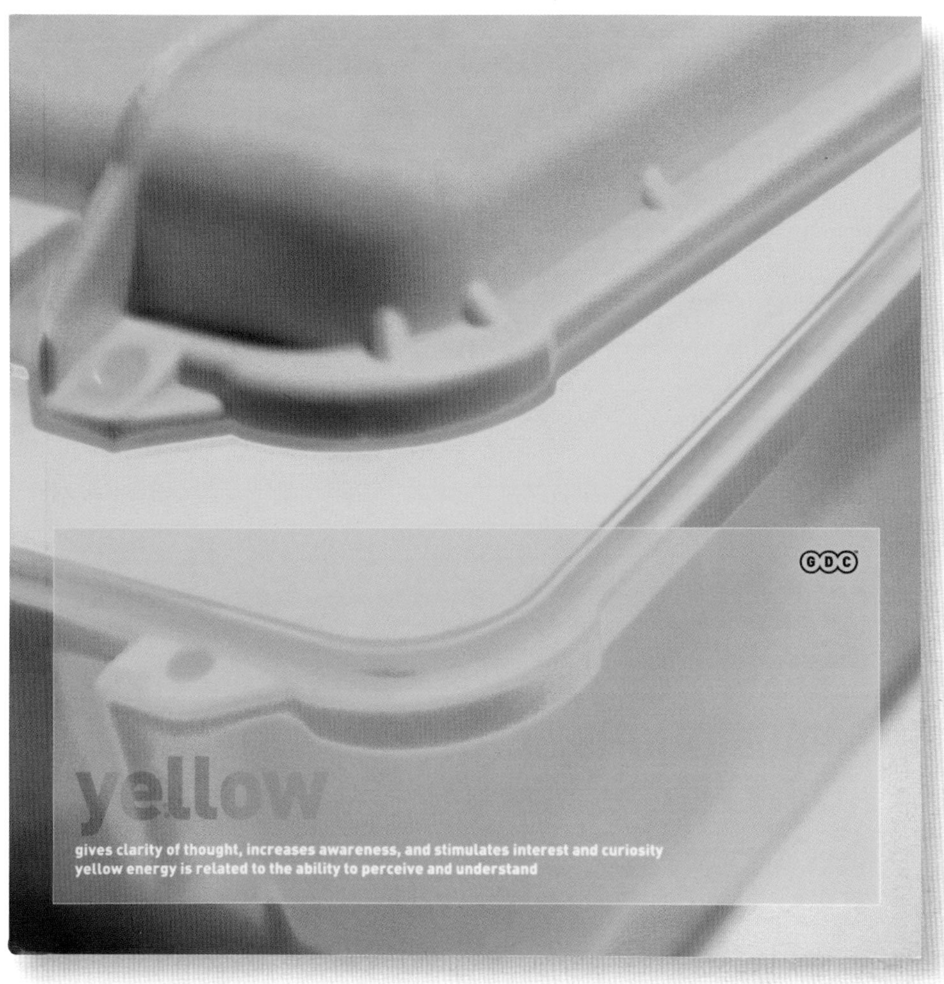

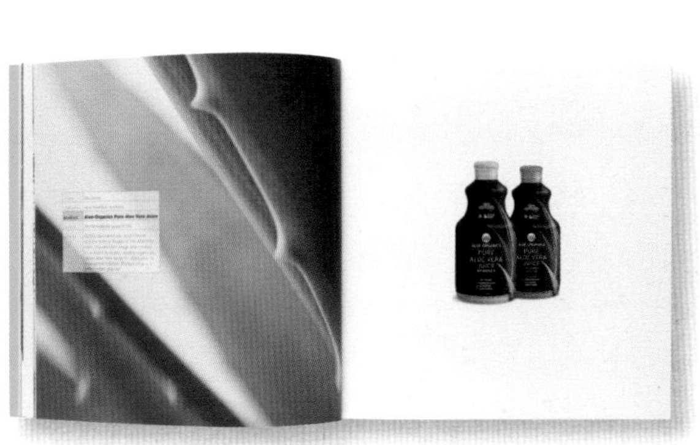

★ **CREATIVE SPARK** | ART DIRECTOR **NEIL MARRA** | DESIGNER **ANDY MALLALIEU** | CLIENT **OZ PROMOTIONS**
PAPER/MATERIALS **COVER: 350 GSM GLOSS, TEXT: 250 GSM UNCOATED OFFSET**

" OZ PROMOTIONS CAN HANDLE EVERY ELEMENT REQUIRED IN HOUSE.. A TRUE 'ONE STOP SHOP' FOR BUSINESSES ACROSS THE SPECTRUM "

Web: www.ozpromotions.co.uk

01

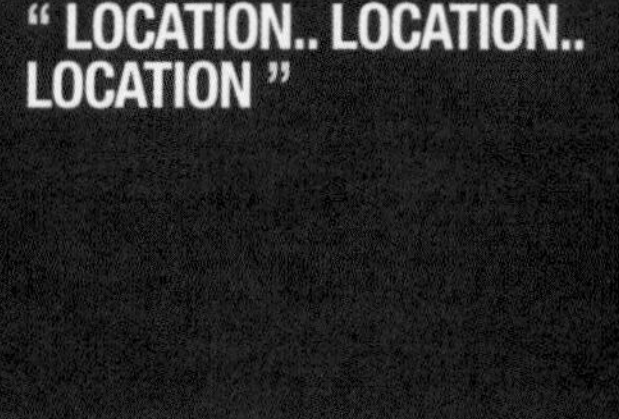

WALLACE CHURCH, INC. | ART DIRECTOR **STAN CHURCH** | DESIGNER **JHOMY IRRAZABA** ★
CLIENT **WALLACE CHURCH, INC.**

★ **GRAPHICULTURE** | ART DIRECTOR **CHERYL WATSON, LINDSEY GICE** | DESIGNER **CHERYL WATSON, LINDSEY GICE**
CLIENT **GRAPHICULTURE**

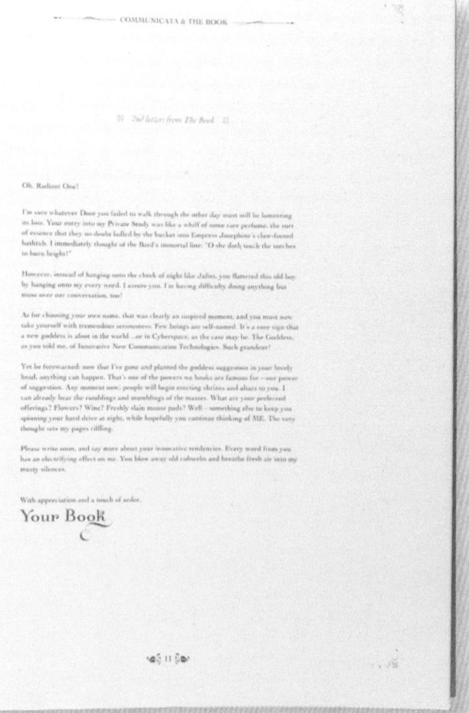
COMMUNICATA & THE BOOK

2nd letters from The Book

Oh, Radiant One!

I'm sure whatever Door you failed to walk through the other day must still be lamenting its loss. Your entry into my Private Study was like a whiff of some rare perfume, the sort of essence that they no doubt ladled by the bucket into Empress Josephine's claw-footed bathtub. I immediately thought of the Bard's immortal line: "O she doth teach the torches to burn bright!"

However, instead of hanging onto the cheek of night like Juliet, you flattered this old boy by hanging onto my every word. I assure you, I'm having difficulty doing anything but muse over our conversation, too!

As for choosing your own name, that was clearly an inspired moment, and you must now take yourself with tremendous seriousness. Few beings are self-named. It's a sure sign that a new goddess is afoot in the world ...or in Cyberspace, as the case may be. The Goddess, as you told me, of Innovative New Communication Technologies. Such grandeur!

Yet be forewarned: now that I've gone and planted the goddess suggestion in your lovely head, anything can happen. That's one of the powers we books are famous for – our power of suggestion. Any moment now, people will begin erecting shrines and altars to you. I can already hear the rumblings and mumblings of the masses. What are your preferred offerings? Flowers? Wine? Freshly slain mouse pads? Well – something else to keep you spinning your hard drive at night, while hopefully you continue thinking of ME. The very thought sets my pages riffling.

Please write soon, and say more about your innovative tendencies. Every word from you has an electrifying effect on me. You blow away old cobwebs and breathe fresh air into my musty silences.

With appreciation and a touch of ardor,

Your Book

11

USA

MIRKO ILIĆ CORP. | ART DIRECTOR **MIRKO ILIĆ** | DESIGNER **MIRKO ILIĆ** | CLIENT **TIHANY DESIGN** ★

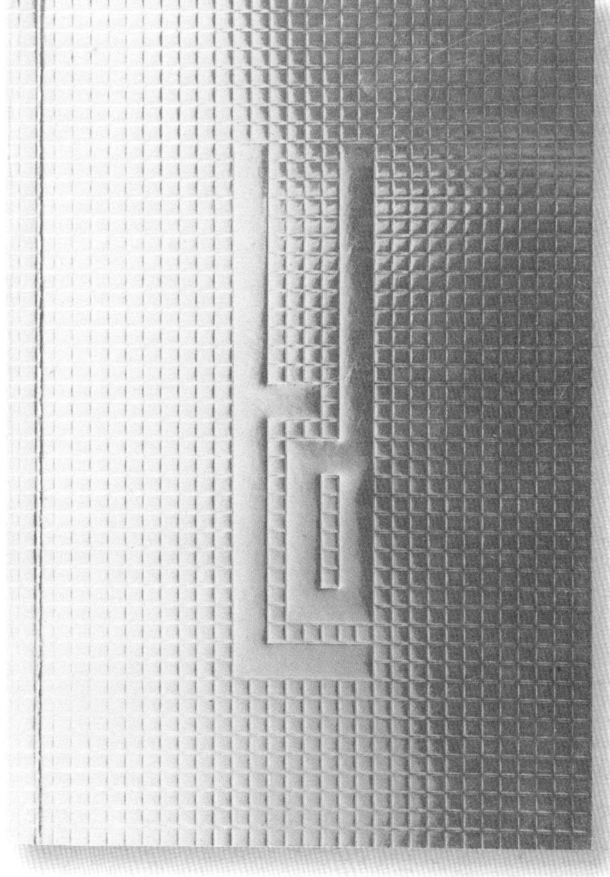

★ **LLOYDS GRAPHIC DESIGN LTD.** | ART DIRECTOR **ALEXANDER LLOYD** | DESIGNER **ALEXANDER LLOYD**
CLIENT **LLOYDS GRAPHIC DESIGN LTD.** | PAPER/MATERIALS **MATTE STOCK, 216 GSM**

LLOYDS GRAPHIC DESIGN LTD. | ART DIRECTOR **ALEXANDER LLOYD** | DESIGNER **ALEXANDER LLOYD** ★
CLIENT **LLOYDS GRAPHIC DESIGN LTD.** | PAPER/MATERIALS **MATTE STOCK, 216 GSM**

★ **PROPELLER** | ART DIRECTOR **DEE FRIEDMAN, ANDI SPEEDY** | DESIGNER **EMILY CARROLL, ANGELA PANIZA**
CLIENT **PROPELLER**

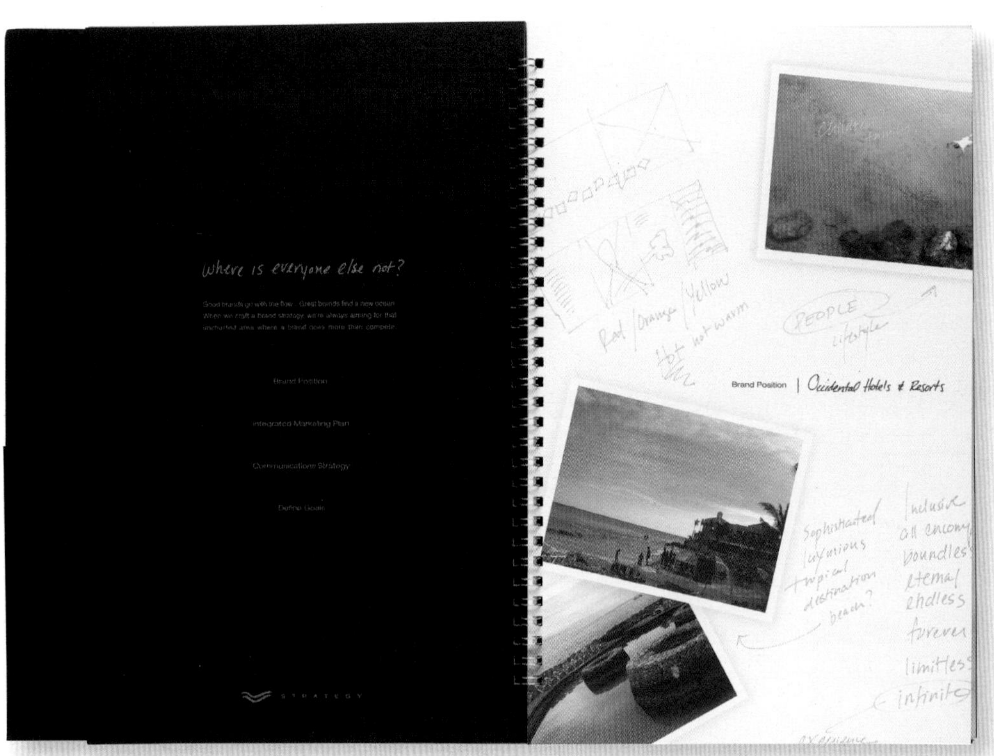

LISKA + ASSOCIATES | ART DIRECTOR **STEVE LISKA, KIM FRY** | DESIGNER **KIM FRY, CAROLE MASSE** ★
CLIENT **LISKA + ASSOCIATES** | PAPER/MATERIALS **120 LB. MCCOY GLOSS COVER, 100 LB. MCCOY GLOSS TEXT**

CHICAGO
BOARD
OPTIONS
EXCHANGE
2005
ANNUAL
REPORT

DAVID CARTER DESIGN ASSOCIATES | ART DIRECTOR **DONNA ALDRIDGE** | DESIGNER **LAUREN BERNDT**
CLIENT **SUSAN KAE GRANT BROCHURE** | PAPER/MATERIALS **PLIKE, SCHEUFELEN, GLAMA, SILKSCREEN, O-RING BINDING**

THIELEN DESIGNS, INC. | ART DIRECTOR **TONY THIELEN** | DESIGNER **TONY THIELEN** | CLIENT **THIELEN DESIGNS** ★
PAPER/MATERIALS **PERFECT BOUND, DIGITAL PRINTING, SCREEN PRINTED CARDBOARD**

THIELEN DESIGNS

TONY THIELEN Tony@ThielenDesigns.com

/// 505 /// 205 /// 3157 ///

Mr. / Ms. Name Placement
XYZ Corporation
1234 Step up to Address
Metro Area, ST 98765
This booklet is a communication piece.

EMPLOYEE OF THE MONTH

MANY FIRMS DOWNPLAY AWARD SHOWS AND PUBLICATIONS. NOT US. WE CONSTANTLY SUBMIT WORK. WE FEEL IT'S IMPORTANT FOR BOTH CLIENTS AND PROSPECTIVE CLIENTS TO KNOW THAT WE DO MORE THAN JUST MEET INDUSTRY STANDARDS. WE EXCEED THEM.

★ **IE DESIGN + COMMUNICATIONS** | ART DIRECTOR **MARCIE CARSON** | DESIGNER **MARCIE CARSON**
CLIENT **IE DESIGN + COMMUNICATIONS** | PAPER/MATERIALS **MOHAWK NAVAJO, STRATHMORE WRITING, TOPKOTE GLOSS**

USA

SAGMEISTER, INC. | ART DIRECTOR **STEFAN SAGMEISTER** | DESIGNER **RADU RANGA** | CLIENT **ANNI KUAN DESIGN**
PAPER/MATERIALS **NEWSPRINT**

★

USA

★ **ANNABELLE GOULD DESIGN** | ART DIRECTOR **ANNABELLE GOULD** | DESIGNER **ANNABELLE GOULD**
CLIENT **DIGITALKITCHEN** | PAPER/MATERIALS **MCCOY**

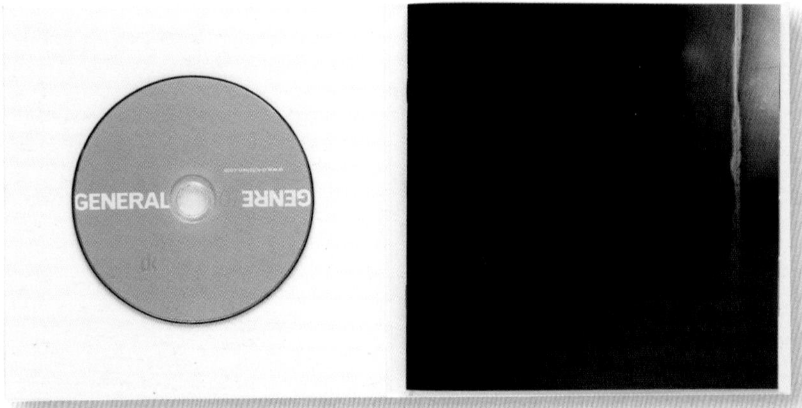

NEO DESIGN | ART DIRECTOR **CRAIG HUTTON** | DESIGNER **CRAIG HUTTON** | CLIENT **ALEX TELFER PHOTOGRAPHY** ★

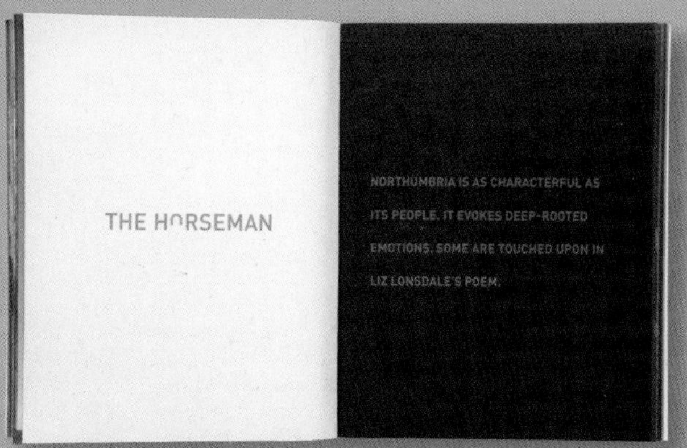

★ IN THIS SECTION

BANDUJO ADVERTISING AND DESIGN

THE JUPITER DRAWING ROOM

PHILOGRAPHICA, INC.

MIRIELLO GRAFICO

SAGMEISTER, INC.

TOKY BRANDING + DESIGN

EDUCATIONAL AND NONPROFIT

★ **BANDUJO ADVERTISING AND DESIGN** | ART DIRECTOR **RYOSUKE MATSUMOTO** | CLIENT **THE FRENCH CULINARY INSTITUTE-**
PAPER/MATERIALS **MOHAWK NAVAJO BRILLIANT WHITE 120 LB. COVER, 80 LB. TEXT**

USA

THE JUPITER DRAWING ROOM | DESIGNER **CARLA KREUSER** | CLIENT **INTERACTIVE AFRICA DESIGN INDABA 10** ★
PAPER/MATERIALS **AVALON MATTE**

PHILOGRAPHICA, INC. | ART DIRECTOR **DAVID HORTON** | DESIGNER **AMY LEBOW**
CLIENT **DEXTER/SOUTHFIELD SCHOOL** | PAPER/MATERIALS **COVER: MOHAWK VIA VELLUM, TEXT: SAPPI MCCOY MATTE**

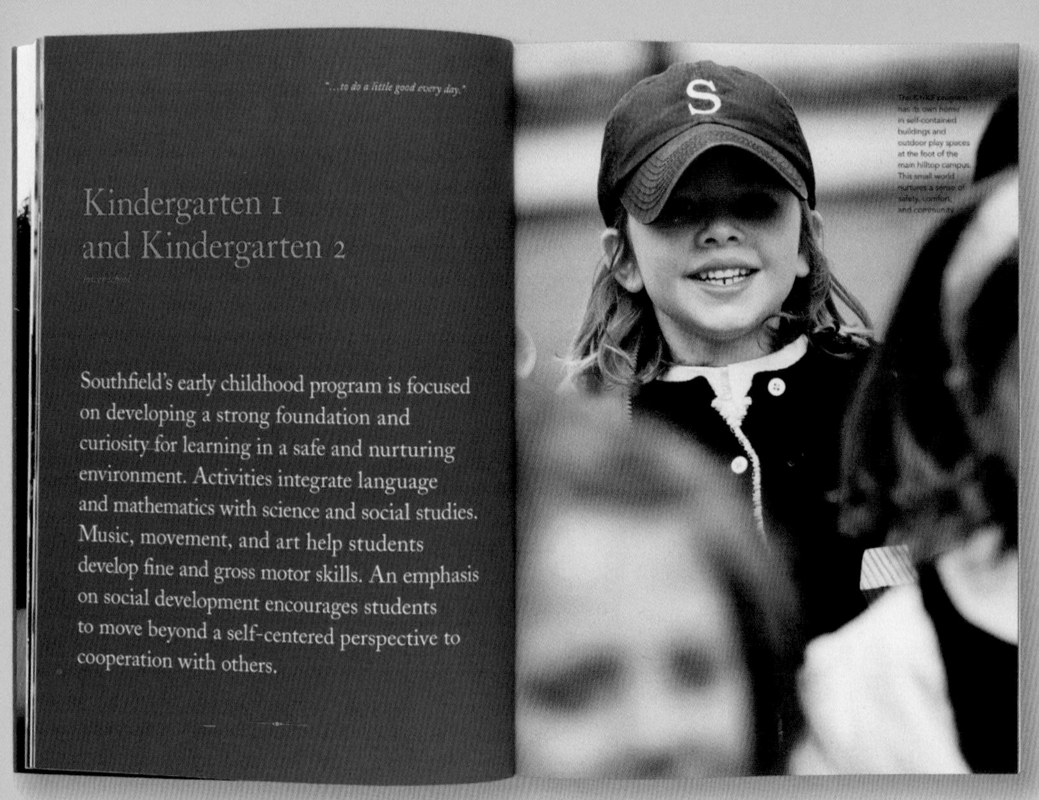

SAGMEISTER, INC. | ART DIRECTOR **STEFAN SAGMEISTER** | DESIGNER **MATTHIAS ERSTBERWER**
CLIENT **COLUMBIA UNIVERSITY** | PAPER/MATERIALS **80 GSM MATTE COATED ART PAPER**

★ **SAGMEISTER, INC.** | ART DIRECTOR **STEFAN SAGMEISTER** | DESIGNER **MATTHIAS ERSTBERWER** | CLIENT **ONE VOICE**
PAPER/MATERIALS **SAPPI COATED**

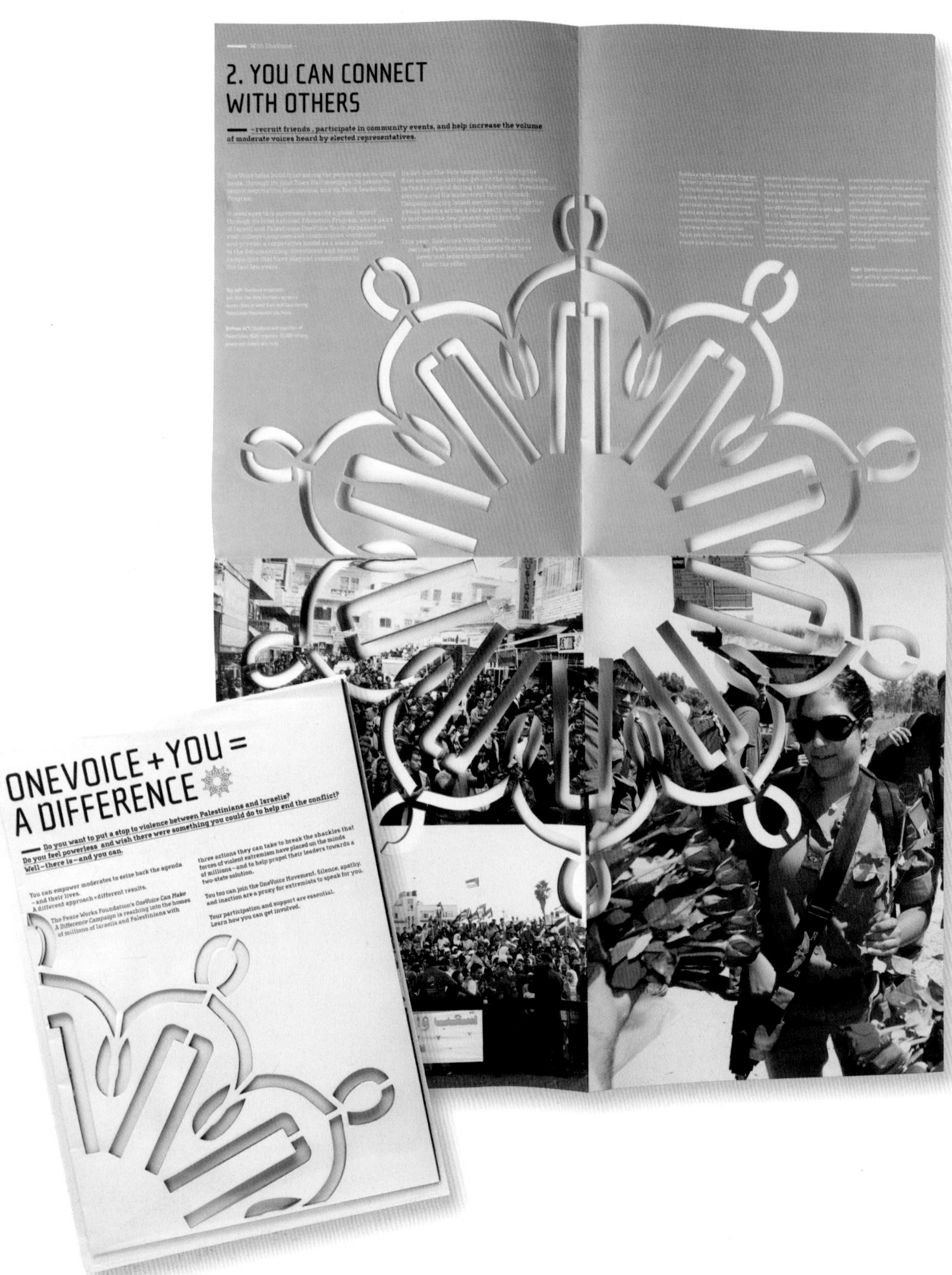

USA

TOKY BRANDING + DESIGN | ART DIRECTOR **ERIC THOELKE** | DESIGNER **TRAVIS BROWN** | CLIENT **ECOURBAN** ★
PAPER/MATERIALS **RUBBER BAND, BAMBOO, RAGLAN BAG**

NEO DESIGN | ART DIRECTOR **CRAIG HUTTON** | DESIGNER **CRAIG HUTTON** | CLIENT **ALEX TELFER PHOTOGRAPHY** ★

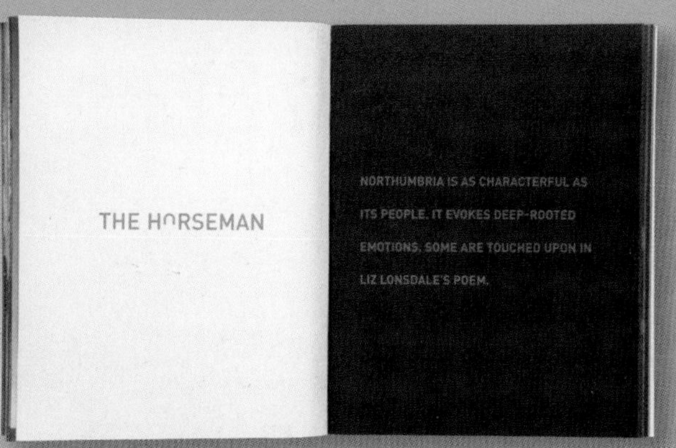

★ IN THIS SECTION

PHILOGRAPHICA, INC. | ART DIRECTOR **DAVID HORTON** | DESIGNER **AMY LEBOW** ★
CLIENT **DEXTER/SOUTHFIELD SCHOOL** | PAPER/MATERIALS **COVER: MOHAWK VIA VELLUM, TEXT: SAPPI MCCOY MATTE**

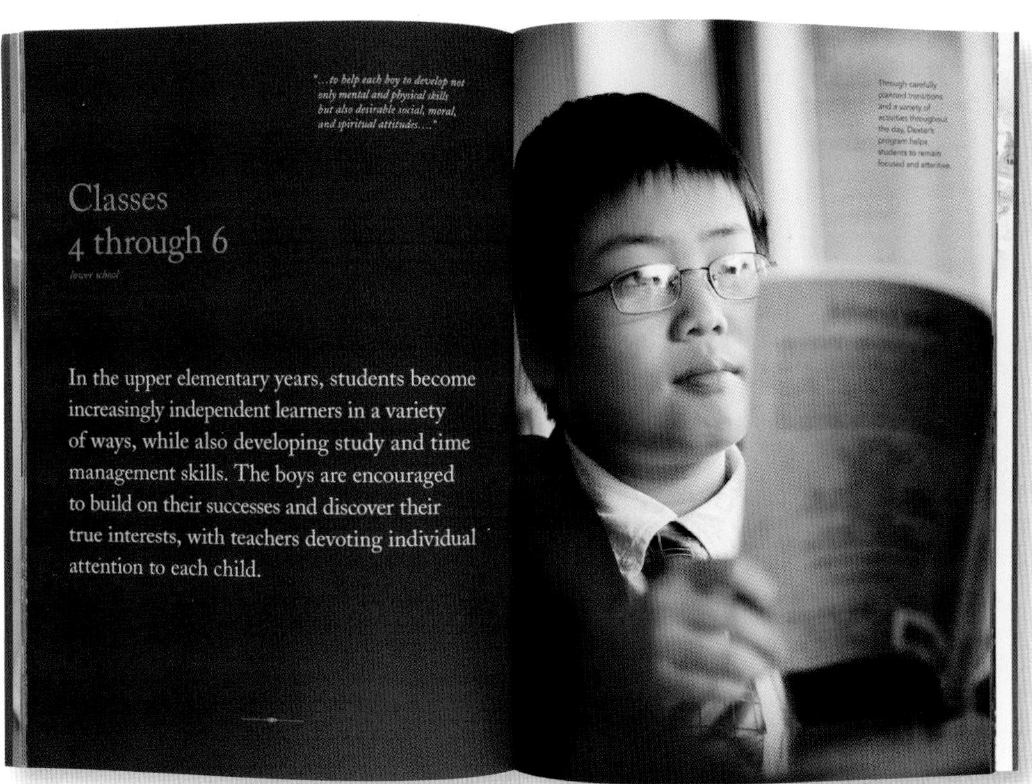

USA

★ **MIRIELLO GRAFICO** | ART DIRECTOR **DENNIS GARCIA** | DESIGNER **DENNIS GARCIA** | CLIENT **SCRIPPS RESEARCH INSTITUTE**
PAPER/MATERIALS **LUSTRO DULL MATTE**

USA

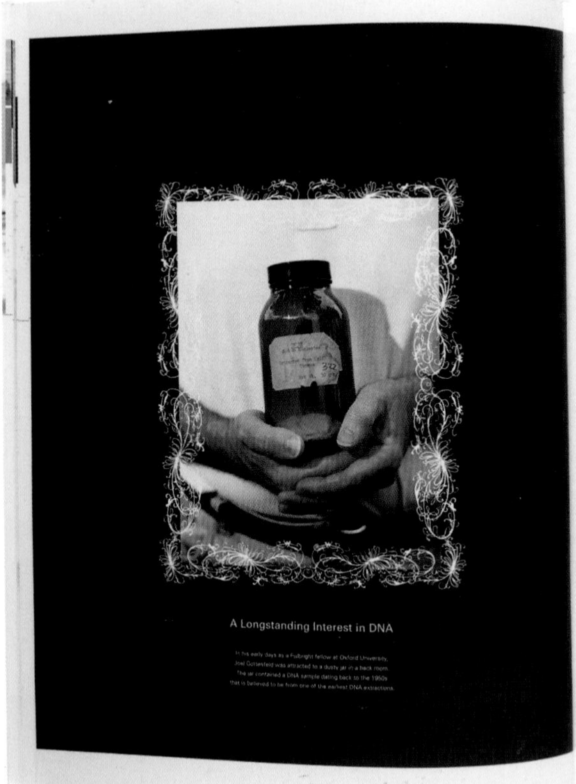

"It's extremely important work. The targeting of specific genes is [Gottesfeld's] approach, and it's a different approach that what everyone else has been doing. It's very promising."

PETER WRIGHT, PH.D

DNA within the cell nucleus. Chromatin is important for relaying transcription information to messenger RNA for recombination and for DNA repair. Bonner theorized that histones, instead of just serving as a structural component of the double helix, actually had an active role in regulating gene function.

"Bonner was one of the first people to recognize the importance of the histone proteins in gene regulation rather than just as a passive glue," says Gottesfeld, whose research still builds on that insight today.

Gottesfeld continued working on chromatin during his doctoral thesis at Caltech, and again at Cambridge, where he landed a postdoctoral fellowship at the MRC Laboratory of Molecular Biology.

His return to Great Britain, this time for three years, gave Gottesfeld the opportunity to meet another influential scientist—this time the godfather of DNA, Francis Crick. Crick was chair of the department in Cambridge, and for about 18 months, the two talked frequently, often about the role of chromatin. While Gottesfeld is an easy-going Southern Californian, Crick could be brash and immodest, sometimes rubbing colleagues the wrong way. Not Gottesfeld.

"He made science so much fun," Gottesfeld said. "He didn't tolerate stupid ideas one bit and he would let you know when he thought you had a stupid idea. And you had to be able to take it. He liked discussions and arguments. I was young and cocky enough to get along with him well."

Crick also helped Gottesfeld get a job at Scripps Research in 1978, where Gottesfeld later became one of the first members of the Department of Molecular Biology.

BUILDING ON BASIC BIOLOGY

Over the years, Gottesfeld has seen his interests evolve from "card-carrying molecular biologist" into a new hybrid that includes a powerful dose of chemistry.

Since the mid-1990s, Gottesfeld has focused on gene expression, more specifically how to bind small molecules that can be synthesized at will to read any particular DNA sequence. This was made possible with a long-term collaboration with Peter Dervan, an organic chemist at Caltech. Their first success came in using this method to find cancer-fighting agents.

"We found a molecule that binds to a DNA sequence in a gene expressed in a wide range of different cancers," Gottesfeld explains. "This molecule turns this gene off. We've identified a molecule that blocks the growth of cancer cells. Using a micro-array experiment, when we looked at a variety of human cancers, we found that the gene was over-expressed in many human cancers, and that this molecule will down-regulate in many kinds of cancers."

Gottesfeld and Dervan have shown the method has efficacy in colon cancer, chronic myelogenous leukemia, and prostate cancer cell lines. Further animal studies are necessary before the molecule can enter human clinical trials.

Using a similar approach, Gottesfeld has been forging ahead with research on Friedreich's ataxia. This endeavor has been made all the more relevant by meeting parents and victims of the disease through the Friedreich's Ataxia Research Alliance (FARA), which has also funded his research.

"These people are grasping at straws for essential therapies," Gottesfeld said. "They are so pleased to find scientists out there working on the disease because it's not well known."

Raychel Bartek, a member of the group and mother of a child suffering from Friedreich's ataxia, has been eagerly following the scientific developments at Scripps Research.

"We know [a therapy] is a long way off," she said from Arlington, VA. "But the whole Friedreich's community is very excited."

DIRECTORY

112-118 50,000 FEET INC.
1700 WEST IRVING PARK ROAD
SUITE 110
CHICAGO, IL 60613
USA
WWW.50000FEET.COM

208 ANNABELLE GOULD DESIGN
7540 MARY AVENUE NW
SEATTLE, WA 98117
USA
WWW.AGOULD.COM
ANNABELLE@AGOULD.COM

176 AUFULDISH & WARRINER
183 THE ALAMEDA
SAN ANSELMO, CA 94960
USA
WWW.AUFWAR.COM
BOB@AUFWAR.COM

142 BANDUJO ADVERTISING AND DESIGN
143 22 WEST 19TH STREET, 9TH FLOOR
212 NEW YORK, NY 10011
USA
WWW.BANDUJO.COM

193 BILLY BLUE CREATIVE
52 LAMBERT ROAD, FLAT 3
LONDON
UK
WWW.BILLYBLUE.COM.AU
JUSTIN@FISHASSOCIATES.COM.AU

036 BLIK
055 655 G STREET, SUITE E
SAN DIEGO, CA 92101
USA
WWW.TYLERBLIK.COM
TYLER@TYLERBLIK.COM

044 BOCCALATTE
507/55 HOLT STREET
SURRY HILLS
SYDNEY, NSW 2010
AUSTRALIA
WWW.BOCCALATTE.COM

107 BONBON LONDON
F5, 13 THE PARAGON
LONDON SE3 OPA
UK
MARK@BONBONLONDON.COM

083-085 BRANDEX
STE. EAST 15 CHESTERFIELD PLACE
NORTH VANCOUVER, BC V7M 353
CANADA
WWW.BRANDFX.CA
SAMANTHA@BRANDFX.CA

086-094 BURTON SNOWBOARDS/SYNDICATE
80 INDUSTRIAL PARKWAY
BURLINGTON, VT 05401
USA
WWW.BURTON.COM

081 CAMPBELL FISHER DESIGN
5013 EAST WASHINGTON STREET, #230
PHOENIX, AZ 85034
USA
WWW.THINKCFD.COM
ER@THINKCFD.COM

014-015 CARRÉNOIR ROMA
028-029 VIA TATA GIOVANNI, 8
ROME 00154
ITALY
WWW.CARRENOIR.IT

057 THE CHASE
160 22 NEWMAN STREET
LONDON W1T 1PH
UK
WWW.THECHASE.CO.UK
STEVE.ROYLE@THECHASE.CO.UK

144-145 CHASE DESIGN GROUP
2019 RIVERSIDE DRIVE
LOS ANGELES, CA 90039
USA
WWW.CHASEDESIGNGROUP.COM

158 CONNIE HWANG DESIGN
185 815 5TH STREET
GAINESVILLE, FL 32601
USA
WWW.CONNIEHWANGDESIGN.COM

095 CREATIVE SPARK
196 116 BURY NEW ROAD
WHITEFIELD, MANCHESTER M45 6AD
UK
WWW.CREATIVESPARK.CO.UK
ANDY@CREATIVESPARK.CO.UK

204 DAVID CARTER DESIGN ASSOCIATES
4112 SWISS AVENUE
DALLAS, TX 75204
USA
WWW.DCADESIGN.COM

096 DECKER DESIGN
14 WEST 23RD STREET, FLOOR 3
NEW YORK, NY 10010
USA
WWW.DECKERDESIGN.COM
COURTNEYC@DECKERDESIGN.COM

108 DEI CREATIVE
159 WESTERN AVENUE WEST, SUITE 450
SEATTLE, WA 98119
USA
WWW.DEICREATIVE.COM

008-009 DESIGN ARMY
030 510 H STREET, NW #200
070-071 WASHINGTON, DC 20002
165 USA
188-189 WWW.DESIGNARMY.COM
PUM@DESIGNARMY.COM

012 DESIGN CENTER LTD.
026-027 KNEZOVA 30
LJUBLJANA SI 1000
SLOVENIA
WWW.CEHOVIN.COM
RUSSIA
OPETRUSHIHA@DESIGNDEPOT.RU

175 DESIGN ONE
53 ASHELAND AVENUE, SUITE 103
ASHEVILLE, NC 28801
USA
WWW.D1INC.COM
175

097-101 DESIGN RANCH
103-105 1600 SUMMIT
126 KANSAS CITY, MO 64108
USA
WWW.DESIGN-RANCH.COM
IS@DESIGN-RANCH.COM

128-129 DESIGNBOLAGET
130-131 RYESGADE 3F, 2ND FLOOR
177-178 2200 COPENHAGEN N
180-181 DENMARK
WWW.DESIGNBOLAGET.DK
DUE@DESIGNBOLAGET.DK

043 DIE TRANSFORMER
IMMERMANNSTASSE 39
44147 DORTMUND/NRW
GERMANY
WWW.DIE-TRANSFORMER.DE

132 ELEVATOR
B. BERISSLAVICA 1
SPLIT 21000
CROATIA
WWW.ELEVATOR.HR

061 EBD
150 2500 WALNUT STREET, #401
183 DENVER, CO 80205
USA
JORGE@EBD.COM

140 ENV DESIGN
ARCHENER STREET 82-84
50674 COLOGNE
GERMANY
WWW.ENV-DESIGN.COM

141 FOLK CREATIVE MARKETING
2A LUKE STREET
LONDON EC2A 4NT
UK
WWW.FOLK.UK.COM
MARK@FOLK.UK.COM

182 GDC-GUGLIELMINO DESIGN CO.
195 33 BAXTER STREET
FORTITUDE VALLEY
BRISBANE, QLD 4006
AUSTRALIA
WWW.GDESIGN.COM.AU
THEPEOPLE@GDESIGN.COM.AU

198 GRAPHICULTURE
22 1ST AVENUE NORTH, 5TH FLOOR
MINNEAPOLIS, MN 55401
USA
WWW.GRAPHICCULTURE.COM

016 HANGAR 18 CREATIVE GROUP
106 220-137 WEST 3RD AVENUE
172-173 VANCOUVER, BC V6J 1K7
CANADA
WWW.HANGAR18CREATIVE.COM

038 HELENA SEO DESIGN
102 2072 SHEFFIELD DRIVE
SAN JOSE, CA 95131
USA
WWW.HELENASEO.COM

206 IE DESIGN + COMMUNICATIONS
422 PACIFIC COAST HIGHWAY
HERMOSA BEACH, CA 90254
USA
WWW.IEDESIGN.COM
KENNY@IEDESIGN.COM

133-134 JKACZMAREK
209 WEST 13TH STREET, #4
NEW YORK, NY 10011
USA
INFO@JKACZMAREK.COM

152-155 JOHNSTON DUFFY
803 SOUTH 4TH STREET, 1ST FLOOR
PHILADELPHIA, PA 19147
USA
MARTIN@JOHNSTONDUFFY.COM

018 THE JUPITER DRAWING ROOM
033-034 3RD FLOOR THE TERRACES
213 BLACKRIVER PARK OBSERVATORY
CAPE TOWN
SOUTH AFRICA
AROSS@JUPITERCT.CO.ZA

067 KARACTERS DESIGN GROUP
185 1600, 777 HORNBY STREET
VANCOUVER, BC V6Z 2T3
CANADA
WWW.KARACTERS.COM
TIM.HOFFPANIR@KARACTERS.COM

045 KIMIKO CHAN DESIGN
2030 3RD STREET, LOFT 10
SAN FRANCISCO, CA 94107
USA
KIMIKO@KIMIKOCHANDESIGN.COM

156 KOLEGRAM
37 ST. JOSEPH BOULEVARD
GATINEAU, QUEBEC J8Y 3V8
CANADA
WWW.KOLEGRAM.COM

123-124 KORN DESIGN
116 SAINT BOTOLPH STREET
BOSTON, MA 02115
USA
WWW.KORNDESIGN.COM
FERNANDO@KORNDESIGN.COM

194 KYM ABRAMS DESIGN
213 WEST INSTITUTE PLACE, SUITE 608
CHICAGO, IL 60610
USA
WWW.KAD.COM
MELISSAD@KAD.COM

127 LISKA + ASSOCIATES
203 515 NORTH STATE STREET, 23RD FLOOR
CHICAGO, IL 60610
USA
WWW.LISKA.COM

200-201 LLOYDS GRAPHIC DESIGN LTD.
17 WESTHAVEN PLACE
BLENHEIM, 7201
NEW ZEALAND
LLOYDGRAPHICS@XTRA.CO.NZ

186-187 LUKAS HUFFMAN
71 WEST 107TH STREET, APT. 5W
NEW YORK, NY 10025
USA
WWW.IR77BOOK.COM

146 MILTON GLASER, INC.
207 EAST 32ND ST.
NEW YORK, NY 10016
USA
WWW.STUDIO@MILTONGLASER.COM

216 MIRIELLO GRAFICO
1660 LOGAN AVENUE
SAN DIEGO, CA 92113
USA
WWW.MIRIELLOGRAFICO.COM

199 MIRKO ILIĆ CORP.
207 EAST 32ND STREET
NEW YORK, NY 10016
USA
WWW.MIRKOILIC.COM

042 NASSAR DESIGN
11 PARK STREET
BROOKLINE, MA 02446
USA
N.NASSAR@VERIZON.NET

051-053 NEO DESIGN
151 4 ST. JAMES TERRACE
209 NEWCASTLE UPON TYNE
UK
CRAIG@NEODESIGN.CO.UK

119-122 NOTHING: SOMETHING: NY
242 WYTHE AVENUE, #7
BROOKLYN, NY 11211
USA
WWW.NOTHINGSOMETHING.COM
WHATISIT@NOTHINGSOMETHING.COM

046 Ó!
ÁRMÚLI 11
108 REYKJAVIK
ICELAND
WWW.OID.IS

109-111 THE O GROUP
259 WEST 30TH STREET
NEW YORK, NY 10001
USA
WWW.OGROUP.NET
KSATROM@OGROUP.NET

031 PAPA INC.
ZLATARSKA 16
ZAGREB 10000
CROATIA
DUBPAPA@INET.HR

017 PETRICK DESIGN
3701 NORTH RAVENSWOOD AVE, SUITE 248
CHICAGO, IL 60613
USA
WWW.PETRICKDESIGN.COM
KLUCO@PETRICKDESIGN.COM

019 PHILOGRAPHICA, INC.
161 1318 BEACON STREET, SUITE 12
162 BROOKLINE, MA 02446
USA
WWW.PHILOGRAPHICA.COM
NIMA@PHILOGRAPHICA.COM

125 PROPELLER
202 1428 BRICKELL AVENUE, 6TH FLOOR
MIAMI, FL 33131
USA
WWW.PROPELLERBRANDING.COM
AMANDA@PROPELLERBRANDING.COM

010-011 RAMP
020 411 SOUTH MAIN STREET, SUITE 615
LOS ANGELES, CA 90013
USA
WWW.RAMPCREATIVE.COM
MICHAEL@RAMPCREATIVE.COM

039 RENEE RECH DESIGN
SAUSALITO, CA 94965
USA
WWW.RENEERECHDESIGN.COM

066 RETHINK
192 700-470 GRANVILLE STREET
VANCOUVER, BC V6C 1V5
CANADA
WWW.RETHINKCOMMUNICATIONS.COM

049-050 RIGSBY HULL
182 2309 UNIVERSITY BOULEVARD
HOUSTON, TX 77005
USA
WWW.RIGSBYHULL.COM

157 ROYCROFT DESIGN
7 FANEUIL HALL MARKETPLACE
BOSTON, MA 02109
USA
JENNIFER@ROYCROFTDESIGN.COM

035 RYSZARD BIENERT
168-170 U. STABLEWSUIEGO 33/9
POZNAN 60-223
POLAND
RYSZAYDBIENERT@YAHOO.PL

148-149 SAATCHI DESIGN
70 GEORGE STREET
THE ROCKS, SYDNEY
AUSTRALIA
MELHUISJ@SAATCHI.COM.AU

174 SAGMEISTER INC.
207 222 WEST 14 STREET
217-218 NEW YORK, NY 10011
USA
WWW.SAGMEISTER.COM

021-023 SALTERBAXTER
056 202 KENSINGTON CHURCH STREET
058-060 LONDON W8 4DP
UK
JWILSON@SALTERBAXTER.COM

037 S DESIGN INC.
135 3120 WEST BRITTON ROAD, SUITE S
OKLAHOMA CITY, OK 73120
USA
WWW.SDESIGNINC.COM

048 SHINE ADVERTISING
159 612 WEST MAIN STREET, #105
MADISON, WI 53703
USA
WWW.SHINENORTH.COM

040-041 SIMON & GOETZ DESIGN
WESTHAFEN PIER 1, ROTFEDER
RING 11, 60327 FRANKFURT/MAIN
GERMANY
WWW.SIMONGOETZ.DE
BVOLLMOELLER@SIMOONGOETZ.DE

136-139 SK+G ADVERTISING
8912 SPANISH RIDGE AVENUE
LAS VEGAS, NV 89148
USA
WWW.SKGADV.COM
TRACY.CASSTEVENS@SKGADV.COM

080 SPRING ADVERTISING + DESIGN
301-1250 HOMER STREET
VANCOUVER, BC V6B 1C6
CANADA
WWW.SPRINGADVERTISING.COM
PERRY@SPRINGADVERTISING.COM

141 SUBSTANCE151
2304 EAST BALTIMORE STREET
BALTIMORE, MD 21224
USA
WWW.SUBSTANCE151.COM
IDA@SUBSTANCE151.COM

076 THERE VISUAL COMMUNICATION DESIGN
LEVEL 1, 16 FOSTER STREET
SURRY HILLS
SYDNEY, NSW 2026
AUSTRALIA
WWW.THERE.COM.AU

205 THIELEN DESIGNS
115 GOLD AVENUE SW, SUITE 209
ALBUQUERQUE, NM 87102
USA
WWW.THIELENDESIGNS.COM

047 TIMBER DESIGN CO. INC.
4402 NORTH COLLEGE AVENUE
INDIANAPOLIS, IN 46205
USA
WWW.TIMBERDESIGNCO.COM

179 TOKY BRANDING + DESIGN
219 3139 OLIVE STREET
ST. LOUIS, MO 63103
USA
WWW.TOKY.COM
ERIC@TOKY.COM

164 TOMATO KOŠIR S.P.
BRITOF 141
KRANJ, 4000, SLOVENIA
WWW.TOMATOKOSIR.COM
TOMATO@SIOL.NET

077-079 ULHAS MOSES DESIGN STUDIO
3/94 RAJNIGANDHA, D N NAGAR, ANDHERI,
WEST MUMBAI, MAHARASHTRA 400 053
INDIA
WWW.ULHASMOSES.COM

064-065 URBANINFLUENCE
3201 1ST AVENUE SOUTH, SUITE 110
SEATTLE, WA 98134
USA
WWW.URBANINFLUENCE.COM
MIKE@URBANINFLUENCE.COM

054 VOICE ADD PTE LTD
406B JOO CHIAT ROAD
SINGAPORE 427634
WWW.VOICE.COM.SG
JASON@VOICE.COM.SG

197 WALLACE CHURCH, INC.
330 EAST 48TH STREET
NEW YORK, NY 10017
USA
WWW.WALLACECHURCH.COM

068-069 WALTERWAKEFIELD
9/96 ALBION STREET, SURRY HILLS
SYDNEY NSW 2010
AUSTRALIA
WWW.WALTERWAKEFIELD.COM.AU

013 WECHSLER
032 6 EMERSON STREET
166 LONDON SE1 904, UK
167 WWW.WECHSLER.COM

147 WICKED CREATIVE
3060 WEST POST ROAD
LAS VEGAS, NV 89118
USA
WWW.WICKEDCREATIVE.COM

073-075 WILLOUGHBY DESIGN GROUP
602 WESTPORT ROAD
KANSAS CITY, MO 64111
USA
WWW.WILLOUGHBYDESIGN.COM

072 WOW BRANDING
101-1300 RICHARDS STREET
VANCOUVER, BC V6B 3G6
CANADA
WILL@WOWBRANDING.COM

About the author

Over the past fifteen years, Perry Chua has applied his strategic thinking to clean, compelling, innovative designs. Although he sees the true reward of his work in the success of his clients, Chua has collected his share of awards from international entities including Applied Arts Awards and Summit International Awards, among others. Chua's work has been featured in over a dozen Rockport Publishers graphic design books, a Barcelona design journal, and a Boston University design textbook titled *Fundamentals of Graphic Design* (Laurence King Publishing, London).

Throughout his career, Chua has developed innovative brand design systems for many clients including McDonald's Restaurants, Mountain Equipment Co-op, Four Seasons Private Residences, Intrawest ULC, and Nokia.

Chua currently resides in Vancouver, Canada, with his wife Lori and their two adorable children. He is the design director at Spring Advertising and Design, and a part-time brand-design instructor at Vancouver Film School.

Chua is also the coauthor of Rockport Publishers' *Logo Savvy: Top Brand-Design Firms Share Their Naming and Identity Strategies*, released in March 2007 and available in bookstores worldwide.